W9-BHY-303

The Mobile Analytics Playbook

A practical guide to better testing

©2016 Commercetest Limited. All rights reserved.

Second Edition
ISBN 978-0-9970694-0-2 (PDF Edition)
ISBN 978-0-9970694-1-9 (Print Edition)

January 2016

TABLE OF CONTENTS

TESTING DISCIPLINES

FOUR PROVEN WAYS TO BOOST APP TESTING

UNDERSTANDING MOBILE ANALYTICS AND FEEDBACK

CONFLUENCE BETWEEN MOBILE ANALYTICS AND SOFTWARE TESTING

YOUR FUTURE

APPENDIX: FURTHER READING

*I would like to thank the following
people who made this work possible:*

*To my Ph.D. supervisors at the Open University,
Arosha Bandara and Sheep Dalton, who have helped
me research the topic since 2012. To the various
friends, colleagues, and companies who have
enabled me to learn, refine, and apply practices in
testing mobile apps. And to the team at Appachhi, in
India, where we're applying various concepts to help
companies improve the testing of their mobile apps
using analytics to drive and improve the testing.*

*To Antoine Aymer who commissioned this book and
ended up helping co-author it. He contributed
personally and also by connecting me with various
leading individuals and organisations in this vibrant
and innovative area of using analytics to improve
our mobile apps and our work.*

*Finally, thank you to the various people who
contributed material, suggestions, and ideas; and
thank you also to the various reviewers.*

- Julian Harty

ABOUT THE AUTHORS

JULIAN HARTY

Julian Harty has been actively involved in mobile apps since 2006 when he joined Google as their first test engineer in Europe and was given the responsibility of testing Google's various mobile apps. Through working at Google he became involved in various test automation frameworks, including various opensource projects such as Robotium,[1] Selenium,[2] and Calabash.[3] He also advises various commercial organisations on ways to improve the qualities of their mobile apps.

Julian's passion is to improve peoples' lives through appropriate use of mobile technologies. He co-created the first Talking Book Reader for Android as a free, opensource project, and he is one of the developers for Kiwix – the offline Wikipedia reader used as an example in this book. He established projects using solar power and Amazon

---

[1] http://www.robotium.org

[2] http://www.seleniumhq.org

[3] https://github.com/calabash

Kindle tablets to help improve teaching and learning in various schools in Kenya, and, more recently created projects using inexpensive computers such as the Raspberry Pi and Android tablets with offline copies of contents from Wikipedia, Khan Academy, and other educational resources.

Julian started his Ph.D. research in 2012 in order to discover how mobile analytics could help improve software testing. The impetus was derived from his experiences of seeing the power of using mobile analytics and some of the current flaws and limitations in how they were being used in major global mobile apps. Julian is one of the long-term contributors to the very popular *Mobile Developer's Guide to the Galaxy*,[4] and he also wrote and published the first book on test automation for mobile apps, *A Practical Guide to Testing Wireless Smartphone Applications*,[5] back in 2008.

One of Julian's goals is to help others become so self-sufficient and capable that they can, in turn, help others to do likewise. This book aims to help you learn as much as you wish about ways to use mobile analytics and complementary techniques to improve what you do and the mobile apps for which you are responsible.

🐦 @julianharty
💼 https://uk.linkedin.com/in/julian-harty-5a010413

---

[4] http://enough.de/en/app-coaching/devguide/

[5] http://www.morganclaypool.com/doi/abs/10.2200/S00219ED1V01Y200909MPC006

ANTOINE AYMER

My friends, colleagues, and peers define me as a passionate market-driven technologist. I started to do product management in 2007, without realising it. Since then, I have been exploring how brands are transforming their business to create new, personal interactions. My research aims at helping mobile teams solve the triple quality-time-cost constraint through innovative testing

strategies. The development of mobile apps makes this equation even more subtle. It is similar to a chess game where developers would inevitably create weaknesses in their position. One use case they forget, one aspect of the experience they overlook, and hours of hard work are instantly turned to dust. Delivering the perfect experience is unfeasible, but we can definitely come close.

Mobile is an amazingly complex topic for which I define QA product scope, develop, and implement global go-to-market plans.

🐦 @AntoineAymer
in https://www.linkedin.com/in/aymer

INTRODUCTION

We all want our work to be meaningful and valuable. Working with mobile apps enables us to reach millions – potentially billions – of users if we create something our users like, value, and find useful.

"Our business branch in 2014 is the 7:01 [train] from Reading to Paddington – over 167,000 of our customers use our Mobile Banking app between 7am and 8am on their commute to work every day."[6] Ross McEwan, CEO, Royal Bank of Scotland.

Today's reality is that mobile apps are transforming businesses. In mobile banking, apps play an increasingly important role in primary bank switching decisions. 60% of smartphone and tablet users report that mobile banking capabilities are "important" or "extremely important" in the decision to switch.[7]

Businesses run on mobile apps – meetings are scheduled, updated, and recorded while on the move and outside the reach of a typical office. Consumers buy using mobile apps, and expect to be able to buy goods and reserve tickets immediately, regardless of network conditions. Apps simply

---

[6] http://www.bbc.co.uk/news/business-your-money-26365616

[7] AlixPartners: "As Consumer Banking Behavior Continues to Evolve, Mobile Is Now Mainstream Says AlixPartners Study", March 12, 2014

need to work! Our challenge is to develop apps that please our users even though many factors are outside our direct control.

Users call many of the shots. They can make or break mobile apps based on their feedback, which is based on their perceptions. They can share their experiences widely and much of their sharing is public and can therefore reach large audiences.

Welcome to this compact book designed to help you learn ways to improve the testing of your mobile apps, particularly using mobile analytics as a key source of information.

USER EXPERIENCE IS EVERYTHING

Users expect mobile apps to work seamlessly, regardless of their choice of technology, their location, or context. They expect mobile apps to be valuable, elegant, and useful, among other things.

Good user experience is moving beyond the app and the single device. People want, and are starting to expect, that they can switch devices and continue where they left off. They expect to transition seamlessly across devices and platforms, e.g., watching a video from where they left off or being able to complete an email draft.

User experience is emotional and is driven by how users think, perceive, and feel. Intimacy, immediacy, and privacy are key factors. Users' perceptions matter tremendously: when they enjoy using an app they will keep using it, tell their friends, and encourage others to also use the app. The qualities of an app have a significant effect on user experience. Good quality software may not be enough to provide a brilliant user experience; however, we can say that poor quality is very likely to adversely affect their experience and memories of that app. Therefore, it is important to measure the various qualities of our apps and improve those that fail to meet expectations. We will describe these qualities later in the mobile testing chapter.

A good user experience is essential to achieving our business goals, whether it is transforming our customers' experience, increasing workforce productivity, or growing revenues. Without effective feedback on this user experience, it is almost impossible to measure the effectiveness of our work and to gauge if we are on track to achieve these business goals.

DOES MOBILE TESTING REALLY MATTER AT ALL?

Mobile apps need to survive ongoing and continual changes of the run-time environment, new devices, new operating system releases, etc. Any and all of these can expose multiple problems with existing apps, which then need to be updated to maintain the status quo. Active apps demand constant care even if the functionality does not change.

In some respects, many of us are now more tolerant of faulty luggage than a defective mobile app from the same company. Users are seldom tolerant of flaws and failures of apps, unless the app is essential to them. According to a recent report, 53% of users uninstall or remove the app in the case of a severe issue, 37% stop using the app, and 28% looked for an alternative.[8]

---

[8] Mobile app use and abandonment: Global survey of mobile app users, HP (January 2015)

Mobile testing is the first line of defence when it comes to diagnosing apps. Essentially, testing helps us bridge the gap between theory and practice, and helps to provide additional information and evidence sooner than we might otherwise receive it.

As you probably know, the initial push is often to get something to work at all, whether that is our app, our mobile testing, our test automation, or anything else new we want to try. The bigger challenge is to find ways to get something to always work, particularly as the users' conditions and contexts change.

Testing mobile apps enables a team to find flaws and problems so that they can be addressed, or mitigated, rather than letting users be the first to find them.

As testing of mobile apps matures, we move from introspective work, such as "Does the code work?", to more valuable and relevant mobile testing. Key considerations include:

- How to better prioritize our development and mobile testing efforts.
- How to reduce or remove irrelevant practices.
- How to keep testing "laser-focused" on user experience and on business success.

TIME TO LOOK AT MOBILE ANALYTICS

Forrester Research calls it the "mobile moment" – that brief instant when users first try your mobile app and decide whether they love it or hate it. Multiple studies confirm that the success of your mobile app – and potentially your business – depends on launch speed, performance, stability, battery usage, and other aspects of the user experience. For example, 55% of users hold the mobile app responsible when they face performance or stability issues, and 53% uninstall or stop using the app.[9]

Mobile analytics provide an easy way to discover how your mobile apps are being used. They are embedded in the app and send small messages containing data to central servers while the app is running and being used. Unlike other sources of information, they potentially cover your entire user-base. The two main exceptions are: when your users choose not to provide information[10] and when there's no network connection to servers that receive and process the data.

Even the standard, often business-oriented, metrics can help us refine and improve our testing. We can also enhance the standard reporting to gather data to help us learn how the app is being used and how it is performing for the end users.

Mobile analytics can be inexpensive to implement and operate. Often the software and reporting are free of charge and easy to implement. However, there are some caveats and limitations, which we will cover in this book to help you choose wisely.

---

[9] Mobile app use and abandonment: Global survey of mobile app users, HP (January 2015)

[10] In some cases, the mobile app or the mobile platform may provide the user with a choice of whether or not they would like to provide analytical data to app developers. For instance, in iOS, Apple asks the user whether they are willing to provide the data to developers when the user commissions the device as part of the setup process. When Julian surveyed software testers the majority wanted the ability to decide whether the data would be provided. Sadly, many apps do not ask the users and simply collect and send the data anyway.

As the usage of mobile analytics increases, we move from simple assessment, such as "Is the app stable?", to a broader perspective where we focus on enhancing the development and testing practices, including:

- How to improve your mobile testing beyond the "shift left" recommendation.

- How to move from traditional "hands-on" testing to the design, analysis, and application of data generated by mobile apps, the users, etc.

- How to use mobile analytics to improve user experience and the quality of our work.

WHAT WILL YOU GAIN FROM READING THIS BOOK?

This book strives to help you, the reader, enhance the quality, velocity, and efficiency of your work by integrating mobile analytics and mobile testing. Furthermore, by harnessing the extra information that is made available, we can also reduce waste in our work and in the apps we ship.

This book unveils ways mobile analytics can help improve mobile apps, particularly the testing aspects of the project. You will learn about 6 ways to help improve app quality:

- Better testing (more skilful, appropriate, and relevant testing techniques.)

- Test automation (tests are run automatically by software.)

- Static analysis (the source code is reviewed and assessed for potential problems.)

- Scaling mobile testing (performing more tests, sooner, exceeding the limitations imposed by interactive testing within a team, e.g., more testing in parallel.)

- Processing and applying feedback from users (e.g., from reviews on app stores, social media, and in-app feedback.)

- Mobile analytics (and similar data emitted from the running app.)

The first four topics are covered in the following chapters on testing, and the remaining two in the confluence chapter. By applying a testing perspective, we will also help you determine the amount of confidence to place in whatever mobile analytics the project decides to use.

HOW READY ARE YOU FOR MOBILE TESTING?

There should not be much debate about the usefulness of mobile testing. We use it as a means to improve the quality of our apps and the associated user experience.

From reading release notes and reviews on app stores, it is obvious that many bugs escape into production without being detected. These then join unfixed bugs found during regular testing. In fact, did you know that crashes and bugs are one of the top reasons for iOS apps to be rejected by Apple?[11]

Worse, these bugs can have a major long-term effect on the apps if they result in poor reviews: for instance, only 15% of users would consider downloading an app with a 2-star rating.[12]

Why is mobile application testing as practiced by many today simply not good enough? And what can we do about it?

---

[11] https://developer.apple.com/app-store/review/rejections/

[12] Walz, A.: The Mobile Marketer's Guide to App Store Ratings & Reviews, Apptentive, 05 May 2015

In this book, we assume you know the basics of testing mobile apps. Therefore, we will only briefly review these different approaches and make recommendations on how to build a cohesive mobile testing framework across multiple disciplines: interactive, functional, and performance. Our first challenge is to understand the scope and dimensions of the rest of the challenges involved in testing mobile apps.

FRAGMENTATION, OR GODZILLA IN THE ROOM!

Fragmentation is probably the scariest impediment to validating the end user experience. The practically infinite permutations impose such a huge challenge to testers that we need to review the fundamentals. OpenSignal[13] detected 24,093 distinct Android devices, illustrated as follows.

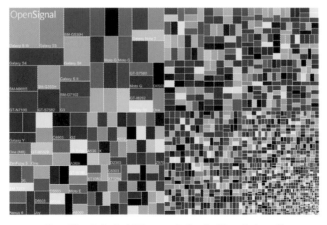

OpenSignal: Android Fragmentation by Manufacturer[13]

---

13   http://opensignal.com/reports/2015/08/android-fragmentation/

Device Characteristics

- Manufacturer (most popular: Samsung, LG, Motorola, HTC, Apple, Microsoft, Blackberry, Sony); for Android, OpenSignal provides a helpful illustration by manufacturer.

- Operating system and version.

- Carrier (Vodafone, EE, AT+T, Verizon, etc.) and type of network connection (Wi-Fi, 4G, 3G, 2G, airplane mode.)

- Class (smartphone, tablet.)

- Physical attributes (thin, small, lightweight.)

- Display dimensions and resolution.

- Multimedia (camera, microphone, speakers, memory card.)

- Sensors (GPS, NFC, Bluetooth, Accelerometer, gyroscope, light, orientation, proximity, ambient temperature, gravity, etc.)

- Built-in technology (battery, ROM, RAM, processing power (GPU, CPU), touch screen, keyboard.)

- Connected hardware (smart watch, headphone, card reader, health gadget, etc.)

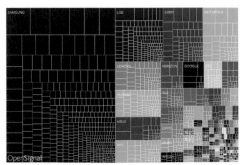

OpenSignal: Android Fragmentation by Manufacturer[13]

13   http://opensignal.com/reports/2015/08/android-fragmentation/

Platform Diversities

The combinations of devices and their operating systems have exploded beautifully as illustrated in the iOS Support Matrix[14] by Empirical Magic Ltd., and Android in the detailed 2015 report by OpenSignal.com.[13]

The platform diversities include the operating systems, and the various APIs available on specific versions of that operating system.

- Operating Systems (Android, iOS, Windows, Blackberry, and trending ones such as Ubuntu, Firefox, Jolla, Tizen.)

- APIs of both libraries and frameworks. System APIs frequently vary from one version of the operating system to another. Sometimes, third-party APIs rely on specific operating system features and may therefore vary depending on the operating system version.

---

13   http://opensignal.com/reports/2015/08/android-fragmentation/

14   From https://iossupportmatrix.com/ released as a Creative Commons Attribution License.

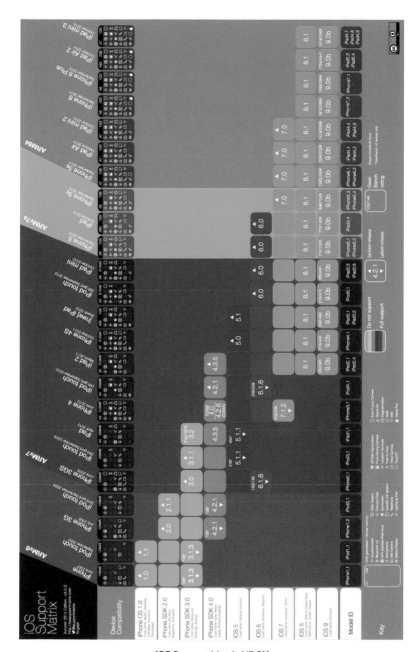

iOS Support Matrix V3.2[14]

---

14   From https://iossupportmatrix.com/ released as a Creative Commons Attribution License.

Fragmentation of Your App

As an app matures, there are likely to be multiple versions of the app installed on users' devices. The app may also be available in "lite" and/or "premium" editions. Users may remain on old versions of an app for a very long time for various reasons. A key consideration is to ensure that any server-side changes, for instance to an API, still work well with older versions of the app.

User's Choices, Settings, and Usage Patterns

Different users have different apps installed on their respective devices. The combination of installed apps can affect the behaviour of other apps, even if they are seemingly unrelated. Each person may have preferences in how both their device is configured and how an app is configured. Finally for this topic, users may have preferences and expectations where they perform a single logical action split across several devices.

- Other apps installed on the device (in particular, numerous web browsers for Android devices.)

- Localization, which may be configured at a device level and/or within a specific app.

- App settings and preferences (user settings for both the app and the device – for instance colour schemes and magnification – can have a significant impact on the challenges of testing to see if the app works with these permutations.)

- Changing network and location.

- Gateway and ports may be disabled or restricted on various networks, for instance on an organisation's Wi-Fi network.

- Multi-channel (apps are part of a larger ecosystem, where users start on one device and continue on another.)

- Interaction (the touch gestures vary by platform and platform version and even the terminology varies.)

- Apple (https://developer.apple.com/library/ios/documentation/ UserExperience/Conceptual/MobileHIG/InteractivityInput.html)

- Android (https://www.google.com/design/spec/patterns/gestures.html)

- Windows (https://msdn.microsoft.com/en-us/library/windows/apps/ hh202911(v=vs.105).aspx)

Fragmentation complicates testing, increasing both cost and time-to-market. Some important questions therefore arise.

- How do we validate our user stories: in the comfort of our lab or in the wild?

- What is our environment of choice to record and replay our test cases: real devices, emulators, or simulators?

- Where do we use test devices: on-premise or in the cloud?

MEASURING QUALITY SO IT CAN BE IMPROVED

There are many ways quality can be measured. Here we will use ISO/IEC 25010:2011 as it is well recognised and clearly identifies many relevant qualities.

Functional Suitability

The functionality of an app needs to meet the expectations of the users as well as providing functions the app owner wants to make available. Mismatches between offering and expectation can cause frustration, confusion, wasted development effort, and ultimately lose users.

Performance Efficiency

Speed matters, as does latency, the sometimes seemingly endless delays waiting for an app to respond or update the UI. Efficiency also matters in order to reduce waste, for instance of precious resources such as network traffic, CPU, memory, battery, and storage.

Usability

Mobile apps cannot afford steep learning curves; after all, many users will only give you one shot before abandoning an app. Even more persistent users are unlikely to appreciate apps that have awkward features (as compared with challenging puzzles or games). Mobile apps also need to be usable on the device and in the contexts in which users find themselves.

Accessibility

As a key aspect of usability, and as mobile devices become more pervasive, people want and need to tailor them to suit their needs, e.g., to change the colour scheme, the font size, or to have the device read out information on the screen. Accessibility support used to be very weak on many mobile devices. It is improving in current versions of the mobile platforms. Our apps need to also improve so they work effectively with the various accessibility features provided by the platforms.

Security

Insecure apps are likely to be discovered, and when they are, their provider loses the trust of the users. That trust is hard to regain, and some users will abandon the app and even stop doing business with that provider. Privacy is a related concern for users, and while some may be willing to allow their data and personal details to be made freely available, many more will have concerns. Companies who consider the privacy aspects related to their apps are more likely to gain and retain the trust of users.

Reliability

Part of apps being dependable is reliability – that apps work whenever the user uses them. Apps also need to be able to provide a reliable and dependable service when things they depend on fail or are unavailable, for instance network connections.

Portability

A measure of how easily software can be used on additional platforms and on additional devices is known as portability. Porting from one platform to another can be a major undertaking, particularly for native apps. Portability from one device model to another varies in complexity; for instance, non-trivial Android apps may have custom implementations to work well on Samsung devices.

Maintainability

Apps need ongoing changes to keep the app viable, particularly because their environment continues to change as new operating system releases and new devices become available.[15] Changes include modifications to fix problems and add new features, in addition to changes to keep pace with new devices and operating system releases. Maintainability is the measure of the quality of the source code and related materials in terms of being able to make these changes.

---

15 Linares-Vásquez, M.: Supporting Evolution and Maintenance of Android Apps, ICSE '14

Compatibility

Apps may need to be compatible with other apps, or APIs. For instance, they may need to be compatible with third-party login authentication mechanisms such as a Facebook logon service or a payment service such as PayPal.

We may also want to consider some characteristics the ISO standard does not mention. These include qualities related to providing apps for a multi-lingual, multi-cultural audience, such as localization and globalization.

As reported in the World Quality Report 2015-16,[16] in 2015, organisations are shifting their attention from more traditional functional and portability testing to include security, performance, ease-of-use, and regression testing.

THE VIRTUES OF VIRTUAL DEVICES

Real devices are more realistic than virtual devices, particularly in terms of testing your apps, as they faithfully reflect the devices users use. There have been conflicting opinions on the value of using virtual devices for testing. However, we have discovered that there are more virtues than many suppose and they are a useful complement to testing using actual devices.

Before we go into the benefits, we would like to clarify some words that get confused: emulators, simulators, and virtual devices. Emulators include the same operating system as the devices they emulate. Simulators look similar to the real devices but do not run the same version of the app; instead, the app is compiled specifically to run in the simulator. Both are types of virtual devices.

---

[16] https://www.capgemini.com/thought-leadership/world-quality-report-2015-16

Android uses emulators. They emulate either the ARM-based versions of Android (most Android devices use an ARM-based CPU) or Intel-based versions of Android. There were other versions of Android in early releases including for MIPS devices; however, these are no longer available.

iOS (iPhones, iPads, etc.) use simulators. To run an iOS app on the computer, the source code is compiled specifically to run in the simulator; that build of the app cannot run on real devices.

Simulators tend to be less realistic in terms of replicating the fidelity of real devices, and will suffer from the same limitations that emulators do; therefore, we will focus on emulators for the rest of this section.

Emulators

When you're keeping up with business demands for frequent, high-quality mobile application releases, any tool that lets you perform testing more quickly and cost effectively needs to be considered.

Therefore, it is only natural that emulators are a hot topic. Clearly, they will be more economical than buying, managing, storing, and securing hundreds of different device and OS combinations. And given that they are virtual, emulators should to be faster at generating feedback into the development lifecycle.

But the ultimate purpose of mobile testing is to replicate and measure as accurately as possible the real user experience. How well can emulators deliver quality for dev/test teams? Emulators do have some limitations that would make them not fully reflective of the user experience. The secret is to understand the use case and how accurate an emulator or real device testing is to understanding the user experience.

We asked GenyMobile, a Paris-based supplier of Android-based application and system services, including an Android emulator. Here's what their product manager, Pascal Cans, wrote back:

> **"** *Even as an emulator editor, we recommend to customers to still test on real devices. The 'feeling' of the user experience and the performance is something hard to measure. Also, some device-specific bugs or hardware-related bugs, cannot be reproduced on emulators.* **"**

That said, there are many positives to using emulators. Pascal highlighted multiple scenarios, which we have incorporated here.

Speed

- Automated non-regression tests can run faster.

- Scale (shorter feedback is always good on a project lifecycle.)

- You can set them up, and reset them, in seconds.

Control

- Emulators may provide greater and easier access to control sensor values, network emulation, GPS location, etc.

Convenience

- Emulators are easy to create with various versions of operating systems as they make compatibility testing of an app on the various actively supported releases, rather than having to upgrade devices. Upgrading devices can be problematic as in some cases there is no easy way to reinstall older versions.

- Any hard-to-prepare testing state can be reproduced easily using snapshots or device cloning – for example, testing an upgrade from an old N-2 version to the new version, N is now easy to test: you just snapshot the old version and upgrade copies of it as much as you need.

- Some sensors are hard to test, for example the battery. With a real device, testing that an app doesn't launch a big background synchronisation process when there is only 5% battery left can be annoying if you have to wait for the battery to deplete sufficiently.

- Custom versions of emulators can be created that have characteristics of unobtainable devices. These can include new screen resolutions as well as other characteristics.

- Going to the aftermarket to buy old devices not produced anymore can be complex in some companies.

- Some devices require convoluted configuration of the host computer before they will connect properly. They may also need device drivers etc. Once your emulator is set up, you can simply use it.

- Testing your app on different network speed/latencies can be hard to set up and control on real devices. They may need SIM cards, carrier contracts, and pricey lab equipment to emulate appropriate network conditions, etc. On an emulator, you just have to select the conditions you want.[*]

---

[*] Although the emulator may lack the fidelity to accurately simulate real network conditions.

Cost

- For a team using a pool of between 30 and 40 Android devices, they may need to replace 30% of those each quarter in order to stay up to date, something which is time-consuming and costly. Emulators can run all the versions of Android and all the screen sizes/density combinations, and they may reduce the need to buy so many devices.

Efficiency

- Instrumentation (emulators can provide relatively good insights of the inner state of the system – CPU, memory, threads state, system logs.)

- For exploratory tests, an emulator can easily monitor and record all events and produce a screen record of the session to help one understand and reproduce unexpected issues. The weakness is the inability to provide feedback on the design and overall elegance of this application.

Limitations of Emulators

Where do emulators fall short? Here are various examples.

Power and Battery

Testing the impact of an app on battery performance is difficult because it depends on so many variables, including how many other apps are running, which ones, and how your app contributes to that ratio. Similarly, how does your app react to a real incoming text message or phone call in the middle of its flow?

Performance

It is important not to overlook the impact of the network on application performance. Emulators use the network connection of the computer, which is often faster and more reliable than mobile connections. Most of the latencies occur on the network, so the difference in the performance characteristics can mask some bugs when testing an app on emulators. However, network virtualization software can emulate slower connections and other networking problems to help redress the balance.

Client-side performance, in particular, tends to be very different when measured on virtual devices and is often not very representative of actual devices.

User Experience

The user experience of using a full-sized keyboard, mouse, and screen to interact with emulators is very different from holding a device in your hands and using it. Problems such as "fat fingers," where people press the wrong button because several elements are too small and close together in the UI on real devices, are seldom noticed on emulators.

Device-Specific Flaws and Bugs

Emulators, with few exceptions, represent general devices, rather than specific ones, so they will not contain device-specific quirks, firmware, libraries, or bugs. Even emulators that resemble specific devices will behave differently. As a piece of history, BlackBerry emulators provided the highest fidelity in terms of replicating actual devices.

As Antoine Aymer discussed in a blog post "For mobile application testing, do you head to the wild or to the lab?",[17] crowd testing an app can complement lab testing, in order to understand how the app responds to different gestures, contexts, and interactions. There are some use cases that are difficult to replicate in a lab, including the more qualitative assessments about UI design. Emulators are a poor facsimile.

The Sweetspot for Emulators and Devices

Emulators are most useful early in the development lifecycle, when used by developers to quickly iterate on developing a new app or new features. They provide fast feedback and most integrated development environments (IDEs) have integrated support for emulators where loading the app to an emulator as soon as the app has been compiled.

During quality assurance (QA) and testing, real devices become much more relevant, in order to see how well the app behaves on a variety of representative hardware. Emulators can still be useful for some aspects of QA but are unlikely to be used for the majority of the testing.

[17]   Aymer, A.: For mobile application testing, do you head to the wild or to the lab? hp.com; revised, 10 Sep 2014

Choosing When to Use Real and Virtual Devices

Mobile testing categories	Real Device	Emulators
Device crashes and errors	✔	✔ [18]
Design/Usability	✔	
Localization	✔	✔
Functional	✔	✔
Regression	✔	✔
Offline/Online	✔	✔
Interruption testing	✔	✔
Interoperability	✔	
Services	✔	✔
Network	✔	✔
Installation	✔	
Performance	✔	

Now that we have covered the testing challenges and have a better idea of how virtual and real devices can help, we can move on to testing disciplines.

---

[18] Device-specific crashes also occur and will have to be found on real devices. However, there are general crashes that can be discovered on virtual devices.

TESTING DISCIPLINES

In this book we are using HP's testing disciplines – interactive, automation, and performance – as ways to test mobile apps. These might be considered as three faces of a triangle where the disciplines are connected and need to be combined to achieve adequate testing. We will discuss each discipline in turn.

FROM MANUAL TO INTERACTIVE TESTING

It may sound curious to consider talking about manual testing, since an Agile mindset encourages us to maximise test automation. However, we still need people to actually test mobile apps in order to capture and assess the human aspects of using the apps, particularly in diverse and potentially unpredictable situations. In addition, there are various limitations in test automation tools, which means that many projects rely predominantly on testing by people, rather than by computer programs.

Nonetheless, there's much room for improvement in how people test mobile apps. Manual testing is still a common term and tends to describe repetitive testing, prescribed by pre-written test scripts on a small number of devices and usage scenarios. It is slow, brittle, and time-consuming to maintain.

More importantly, prescriptive, repetitive, manual testing fails to find bugs caused by rich interactions, combinations of circumstances, and so on. Manual testing is shifting from following prescriptive test cases to being more interactive because of the complexity of assessing the human aspects of using the app realistically on mobile devices. It becomes extremely effective when it comes to understanding the "unpredictable" effect of mobile usage and providing the human sentiment on the overall look and feel. The term we use here is *interactive testing*.

Using Heuristics

Several thought-leaders have created testing heuristics. These heuristics often include several of the quality factors and they help to encourage testers to remember to test their mobile apps more comprehensively. They have achieved good results in terms of helping focus testing. Although heuristics are fallible, they provide a good structure to guide the testing of mobile apps by defining critical risk areas to consider and test. Here are several mobile-specific heuristics.

- **I SLICED UP FUN**[19] is a useful and easy-to-read article covering many aspects of testing a mobile app. This is one of the early heuristics, from 2010, yet still applicable.

- **COP FLUNG GUN**[20] introduces six additional aspects (and misses out others) from "I SLICED UP FUN". The additions include Gestures, Location, and Updates.

- **FISH TANK**[21] focuses on testing through the development lifecycle.

---

[19] *Kohl, J.: Testing Mobile Applications with I SLICED UP FUN! http://www.kohl.ca/; 2010.

[20] Moolya Testing Blog: A mnemonic mobile app model, 06 May 2014.

[21] Dhanasekar, S.: Fish Tank, a Test Model for Android and iOS apps, 08 Jan 2015.

- **Empirical Development of Heuristics for Touch Interfaces**[22] includes a useful comparison of differences between testing for "fat fingers" on emulators and on actual devices. Another relevant article on testing mobile apps is Heuristics for Evaluating Mobile Designs.[23]

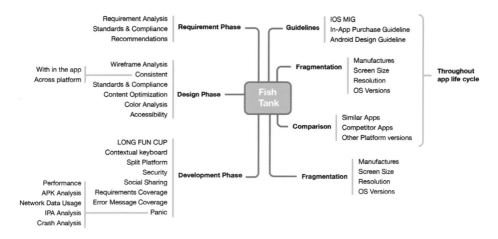

FISH TANK Mindmap, used with permission from the author, Dhanasekar[21]

Heuristics are predominately used during interactive testing sessions. They can also be used more generally, for instance as reminders when designing automated tests. A good place to learn about heuristics is from Mike Kelly who started using them over a decade ago; see http://michaeldkelly.com/blog/category/heuristics.

21 Dhanasekar, S.: Fish Tank, a Test Model for Android and iOS apps, 08 Jan 2015.

22 Baker, R. and Sun, X.: Empirical Development of Heuristics for Touch Interfaces, 02 Jun 2014.

23 Heuristics for Evaluating Mobile Designs, last edited: 03 Nov 2014

Using Personas

Mobile testers should consider using a variety of distinct personas (or profiles) to validate the user experience with different mindsets. Personas are a well-established practice in software testing. Each persona is modelled on a distinct, characteristic user of the app. Testers can assume the characteristics of that user as a role play where they try to think and act as that persona would. Antoine Aymer wrote a useful article on using multiple mindsets to test mobile apps.[24] Personas can be based on interviews, user-provided feedback, and/or analytics. During interactive testing, a tester may use several personas to add variety. Through doing so, they are likely to find more issues than simply being "themselves".

Interactive testing can be performed in the lab and beyond the lab.

Interactive Testing in the Lab

"In-the-lab" testing refers to activities that take place in an organisation (or outsourced) as part of their application development lifecycle.

Testers can either interact with a device in their hands or connect to one available in a remote location. Some manual testing tools can automatically record the actions performed in the GUI. They can also provide annotated screen captures, movies, and device parameters. Testers can incorporate additional feedback on their perceptions and experiences about using the app. This information can accelerate collaboration between the development and quality assurance teams, enabling faster defect resolution and eradication.

---

[24] Aymer, A.: Mobile App: Into the mindset of a manual tester engineer (part 1), 05 Sep 2014.

Interactive Testing Beyond the Lab

The main challenge that in-the-lab practices fail to address is how to incorporate user experience into the overall testing effort. We can scale our testing beyond what we can achieve with in-the-lab capabilities by involving people outside our company, such as crowdtesters and early adopters. As Antoine Aymer concludes in a blog post,[25] in-the-wild testing is not an alternative to in-the-lab testing but a complementary practice. Mobile apps can be distributed using platform-specific mechanisms (e.g., TestFlight) or by using enterprise-oriented distribution tools. Crowdtesters can be employees or external testers. They provide greater variety than practical in the lab, for example:

- Expert testing of additional locales.
- Greater variety of usage conditions.
- Variety in interactive testing.[26]

Early adopters are users who opt-in to use (and hopefully test) early releases of an app. They need to be willing to take partly baked releases and use them. Also, many will provide more feedback than typical users, where that feedback can be (1) acted on before the mainstream release or (2) kept distinct from feedback of the "hardened" (or improved) mainstream release. They may be supported via the app stores, and possibly additional feedback channels.

Facebook may have adopted an additional intermediate approach, where employees are now required to use Android devices[27] so they more closely

---

[25] http://h30499.www3.hp.com/t5/Application-Lifecycle-Management/For-mobileapplication-testing-do-you-head-to-the-wild-or-to-the/ba-p/6474844#.VhLizbRVikp

[26] Baker, R. and Sun, X.: Empirical Development of Heuristics for Touch Interfaces, 02 Jun 2014.

[27] Tung, L.: Facebook reveals why it's forcing workers to swap iPhones for Android; 30 Oct 2015.

reflect the experience of end users, and where they have the option to use slow connections that more closely reflect reality for users in emerging markets.[28]

THE MANDATE FOR AUTOMATION

Test automation has been touted as essential for coping with the speed of agile development projects. There are tens of choices of test automation for mobile apps, including tools provided with the software development kits, opensource, and commercial products. Some of these tools evolved from desktop and/or web test automation, while others have been developed specifically to test mobile apps.

Test automation software performs the testing. Automated testing can use various ways to interact with the mobile app, including object recognition, image-based recognition, using coordinates, and custom test automation APIs integrated into the app. They may also include generating, or synthesising, various inputs, which are sent to the app for the app to interpret and process.

There are various perspectives on what automation means in the context of testing. For some, it means the tests are fully automated software programs that interact either with small subsets of the source code (commonly called "unit tests") or by interacting with the GUI of the mobile app. For others, test automation is more of a continuum, where aspects of the testing, such as preparing the configuration and capturing the results are automated, but the testing is performed interactively.

---

[28] D'Onfro, J.: Facebook will give employees super slow internet speeds every Tuesday to better understand markets like India; 27 Oct 2015.

Current test automation software have limitations in the way(s) they interface with the device and the app. For instance, most approaches only interact with the GUI. Few support audio input or input to other sensors, so – for example – they would not be able to test audio or replicate a shake gesture.

They also have limitations on what they can assess in terms of the behaviour or outputs of the app running on a mobile device; for instance, the perceived quality of video playback, or whether the GUI layout is as desired on the various devices. Later in the book, we introduce the concept of test automation interfaces, which help us to learn the ways test automation software interfaces with what it is intended to test.

It is often possible for developers to create specific test automation to exercise particular aspects of their mobile app. For instance, one of the authors was part of a team that devised ways to test a "voice search" mobile app using a custom version of the app. The custom app replaced the standard GUI with a basic UI that was able to use prerecorded audio files as inputs to the core application logic. The app needed to send duplicate network packets to counter various types of packet loss in mobile networks. Testing the app by hand would have been too slow and would have had undesirable variations in timing. However, most organisations don't want to get as involved in crafting specific test automation.

Shopping List Considerations

There are various factors to consider in order to pick tools and/or frameworks for your mobile app. Here are some of the key motivators.

- Where we are willing and able to "spend". Some of us are willing to dive in, write code, and implement whatever it takes to use test automation. Others may not have the technical skills, or may not want to spend time dealing with the details of getting test automation working and keeping it working. Some may have restrictions on the amount they can pay for licenses, external support, etc., and therefore have to find and use inexpensive or free options. Similarly, for some teams and organisations, latency may be a major factor where delays in resolving test automation challenges are very expensive, perhaps more expensive than paying for premium support. Finally for this topic, the ability to influence the product's, or tool's, direction may be a key consideration. Again the investment of time, money, and energy are worth considering.

- **Technical Aspects:**

  - Richness of inputs, controls, and interactions.

  - Scope or extent by which you can control the devices; for instance, you may need to test across several apps, and/or control the configuration of the device. However, these capabilities are not supported by many of the automated testing frameworks.

  - The platforms and technologies that need to be supported: a first pass is to consider the platform, for instance iOS, Android, Windows Phone, etc. However, the technologies used to implement the app are also important, particularly where they use a web browser as part of the app, such as a WebView in Android or iOS. Some mobile test automation tools do not interact effectively with what's happening in the web browser, which could mean major aspects of your app are not able to be tested with that tool.

- ○ Portability of test scripts across devices, releases, and as aspects of the GUI change.

- Ability to find bugs you can and want to address.

- Aspects that the tests are intended to address.

Test Automation in the Lab

There are several topics worth considering, including:

- The choice and quality of the Test Automation API (which may be implicit and informal, or more concrete and formally provided as/for an app.)

- Limits and limitations in the reach and control provided by the Test Automation tool/framework/API/Interface/etc., e.g., few provide access for audio input.

- The ability to control the run-time context, both on the device, and beyond the device's boundaries. Similarly, the ability for automated variation of responses[29]/inputs[30] can help improve the quality and value of the tests. Sometimes we may have automated testing and automated variations in the context, while other times we may automate one and perform the other interactively.

---

[29] For network protocols, API responses, etc.

[30] For sensor values, etc.

Test Automation Beyond the Lab

There are at least a couple of ways that automation can help test beyond the lab. These include data-gathering apps and probes.

Data-Gathering Apps

Apps that explicitly (and with the user's knowledge and agreement) gather data in various ways. This data may be across all other apps, for instance tracking calls and network traffic per app, etc. They can also gather more detailed information than mobile analytics libraries typically obtain/provide.

An example of a commercial data-gathering app is Shunra's Network Catcher,[31] which explicitly transmits and receives data on the network's performance characteristics in order to provide that information to the user. The app also obtains details of the device's location and network connection. The data is then used as a profile that testers can use to configure a virtual network to enable them to test the app using a fairly realistic profile that resembles real-life network conditions.

An example of a research-focused app is Device analyzer.[32] Users opted-in to using the app, which collected many facets of data, including location, signal strength, battery levels, and usage data. They discovered considerable diversity in behaviour between users and also over time. The app is available for custom experiments as is the data for people who want to do their own analysis.

---

[31] https://play.google.com/store/apps/details?id=com.shunra.nce&hl=en

[32] More information is available in the related academic paper titled: "Device analyzer: Understanding smartphone usage"

They have collected over 100 billion records from over 17,000 devices. More information on the project is available at http://deviceanalyzer.cl.cam.ac.uk/.

Probes

There are various services available to monitor the behaviour of an app (and/or the underlying internet-based services) where the services are distributed. The "testing" may be superficial in terms of functionality; instead they focus on latency and availability of the app and related services.

PLEADING PERFORMANCE IN THE COURT OF USER EXPERIENCE

Few would argue that we have become the most impatient users of all time. Slow apps are abandoned and get uninstalled. The speed of an app is subjectively measured by users using various criteria, including the time taken for content to be seen on the screen (for example when the app is launched) and the time taken for the app to respond to inputs from users.

Mobile performance testing is a complex discipline for several reasons. In particular, performance testing and assessing performance tend to be more in-depth and technical than the other disciplines.

> The overall architecture of both the app and related servers need appropriate performance requirements for their various aspects.

- The front-end performance, i.e., the mobile app, needs to include the right balance of type of device, OS, apps running in the background, processing power, memory, battery, and storage. (Back to the challenges of fragmentation!)
- The network has a huge impact on performance. *"Consider that a typical PC takes 30 ms to connect to a server,"* explains Todd DeCapua, TechBeacon's chief technology evangelist, *"whereas it takes a mobile device typically 300 ms to connect. That is a 10x slower connection. The result is a 50 percent increase in your back-end infrastructure. If you are already running at a 65 percent utilization for your PC traffic and then add just five percent mobile traffic, you will crash your data center".* [33]

- Servers that interact with a mobile app also need comprehensive performance testing. The testing may include a mix of mobile apps on real devices, mobile apps on virtual devices, and simulated network traffic from load generators. The location of requests and their network connection (as mentioned earlier) may also be important factors to consider in the test plan.

- Some tests involve replicating a series of connected API requests that clients would make when interacting with server-based APIs, in order to validate cross-platform performance.

Focusing on the user-centric aspects of mobile performance testing involves aspects such as responsiveness and ensuring the app is written and able to multi-task in ways that meet the user's expectations of responsiveness. When the app is not yet responding, it's effectively dormant from a user's perspective.

---

[33] As quoted in David, M. The essential guide to improving mobile performance, Oct 2015

Google has published the RAIL Performance Model[34] for Chrome. The concepts are also relevant for mobile apps. RAIL represents: **R**esponse, **A**nimation, **I**dle, **L**oad; Google's model explains each of these in more detail.

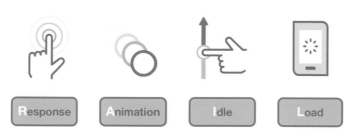

Google's RAIL Performance Model[34]

In terms of systems and software engineering, mobile performance testing can include aspects such as threading models, scalability, load balancers, traffic prioritisation, etc., and as such is often performed by specialists dedicated to the topic.

Performance Testing in the Lab

For mobile performance testing in the lab, people often use a hybrid where they use several real devices to collect realistic, end user-oriented timings. These timings help calibrate timings from generating large volumes of network requests to load up the various servers and related infrastructure needed to support the overall user-base and service.

---

34 Based on Google's RAIL Performance Model https://developers.google.com/web/tools/chrome-devtools/profile/evaluate-performance/rail

Real Devices

For real devices, there are a couple of key considerations. These include:

- The fidelity of the tool in terms of being able to generate desired performance profiles and capture accurate results.

- Deciding what measurements and observations to use to assess "performance".

Virtual Users

For virtual users, the requests aren't being generated on real devices; instead, representative network requests are sent in parallel from many "virtual users". The tests may be run on a local network or over a mobile network.

Performance Testing Beyond the Lab

The focus here is on ways to gather performance data when the app is being used beyond the lab. Mobile analytics can be an excellent way to gather and send data when there's a suitable low-latency, inexpensive, and reliable connection to the mobile analytics data collection services/servers.

User-Provided Perceptions and Data

Users could be asked to provide feedback on perceived performance, satisfaction, etc. There are examples of research in this area, e.g., by Orange.fr for mobile video streaming as part of their Quality of Experience (QoE) research.[35]

SUMMARY OF THE TESTING DISCIPLINES

We have now covered interactive, automation, and performance testing disciplines in and beyond the lab. It is time to move on to proven ways to improve testing of mobile apps.

FOUR PROVEN WAYS TO BOOST APP TESTING

We have already introduced various concepts and approaches to improve the testing of mobile apps. Through reviewing several hundred research papers and the state of the art in the industry, we have identified four well-accepted and proven ways to boost mobile app testing. They are:

1. Better testing.

2. Test automation and continuous automated testing.

3. Scaling testing.

4. Static analysis.

We will cover these in turn.

1) BETTER TESTING

When testers apply better practices and techniques, they can test more effectively. Often the concepts seem too simple to work. For instance, using personas and heuristics are not complex or complicated to try. Nonetheless, when people aren't aware of these techniques or do not apply them, their testing can be mediocre. For instance, only 30% of screens and 6% of the code were exercised by 7 users who tested 28 popular Android apps.[36]

Also, when testing is limited to the lab it lacks the richness, realism, or variety of how the apps are actually used. Furthermore, learning how to understand the information available on the device and the tools that access that information will enable testers to use these rich seams of data.

We want to find breaks in the system before users do. One way to achieve this is to introduce volatility into the system and environment. We can embrace *"disorder, randomness, and impermanence to make systems even better"*,[37] where the system is the mobile device, the network connection, and other services the app relies on. The same book makes two key points well worth considering when designing and performing our tests: *"How to use continual experimentation and minor failures to make critical adjustments – and discover breakthroughs"*, and *"How an overreliance on measurement and automation can make systems fragile"*.

[36] As research discovered: "Relying on end users to conduct the exploration might not be very effective: we performed a 7-user study on popular Android apps, and found that the combined 7-user coverage was 30.08% of the app screens and 6.46% of the app methods." People don't necessarily cover much of the functionality of apps when testing ad-hoc. (However, we would expect interested and engaged testers to do better than the participants in this study.) (Azim, T. and Neamtiu, I: Targeted and Depth-first Exploration for Systematic Testing of Android Apps. University of California, Riverside, 2013)

[37] Zwieback, D.: Antifragile Systems and Teams, O'Reilly; Apr 2014

TBS

Testing software actually consists of at least three primary activities: **T**esting, **B**ug investigation, and **S**etup (TBS). Time spent on setup and bug investigation effectively reduces the time needed for doing the actual testing. As the TBS figure shows, we want to increase T and reduce the B and the S.

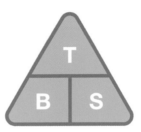

TBS Diagram

TBS is one aspect of Session-Based Test Management (SBTM), both the work of Jon Bach, a well-recognised guru in software testing.

Recreating Sufficient Fidelity

Tests don't necessarily reflect reality, particularly when testing mobile apps. Our environment, device, conditions, experience, test design, and many other factors affect the validity of the results in terms of whether the bugs would be relevant for end users, and how completely we can capture problems that would affect these users.

> Conversely, as we work to improve the fidelity of our tests and
> our testing we risk over-investing in time, effort, and money.
> Therefore, it's useful and important to find ways to test with
> sufficient fidelity to find flaws that are particularly relevant to
> various stakeholders, including the end users.

Improving the setup time and bug investigation can also indirectly help improve the testing and the ability to analyse, and reproduce, what happened.

Improving Setup Work

Installing apps and configuring devices can be burdensome and time-consuming. We can automate the creation and distribution of test releases of the app, for instance, using the opensource Continuous Integration tool: Jenkins.[38] Another opensource project, Spoon,[39] focuses on making automated tests easy to distribute, observe, and run.

Some smart teams have also created small software utilities that enable them to change system settings such as the locale, Wi-Fi, etc. Android's open architecture enables these apps to be written, installed, and used more easily than for other mobile platforms which are more "closed" in terms of what third-party software is permitted to do.

---

[38] https://jenkins-ci.org/

[39] https://github.com/square/spoon

Improving Bug Investigation

Chasing bugs can be extremely frustrating and time-consuming. Also, critical information can be lost in the communication between the finder of the bug (which may be software) and whomever is trying to understand and possibly recreate the problem. Improving the bug investigation reduces the latency and cost of being able to make informed decisions of what to do about the bug.

There is plenty of information written to the central log on mobile devices. Log gathering, filtering, and processing can enable these logs to be analysed quickly, accurately, and reliably.

GUI screen recorders, cameras, screenshots, etc. provide useful information on the GUI aspects of an app. There is a helpful, practical article on using various camera and recording software for low-cost usability testing.[40]

We may need to test on several particular devices to hone in on specific bugs. In the confluence chapter, we will elaborate on effective ways to select a suitable set of devices to test on.

2) TEST AUTOMATION AND CONTINUOUS AUTOMATED TESTING

Test automation is one of the most popular ways trying to improve testing of mobile apps, and there are a plethora of potentially suitable products and frameworks available. Once the automated tests exist, they can be run more frequently than human testers could achieve from a practical perspective.

---

[40] Mason, D.: Usability Testing for Mobile Devices; code7.co.uk; 17 Nov 2014.

Also, they can be run when testers aren't available; for instance when the app is updated overnight and the testers have finished work for the day.

Continuous automated testing is where the tests are run automatically when the source code for an app has been updated and compiled successfully. The automated tests can provide lower-latency, consistent feedback to the developers and therefore enable them to investigate problems that, overall, have been reported sooner than would be practical with interactive testing. They also provide "some testing" each time the source code is compiled successfully; therefore, they provide more traceability and early warning of failures they detect.

There are a couple of additional concepts worth understanding to use test automation more effectively. These include the test automation interfaces and test monkeys.

Test Automation Interfaces

Regardless of the choice of test automation, that automation needs to interact somehow with the app it's intended to test. There will be at least one test automation interface, possibly several. These may be officially and publicly supported, ad hoc, or a custom interface embedded in the app.

The choice of test automation interface can have a massive effect on the ease and effectiveness of the test automation. For instance, if they are informal and reverse-engineered by a testing team, then many changes by developers of the app may require emergency changes to the test automation scripts. Sometimes, simple techniques such as adding specified labels to key GUI elements can significantly improve the reliability of the test automation as the underlying software changes while also reducing the maintenance effort needed to maintain the current automated tests.

Of the development teams who actively support automated tests, many include a private test automation API built into their mobile app. This API provides access to internal data and often includes commands to interact with the app.

More information is available in an extended article.[41]

Test Monkeys

Test monkeys are automated programs that can help test your software. Monkeys are available to test the GUI. For instance, Android's Monkey[42] has been available since very early versions of Android and has helped find many bugs that shouldn't exist, but do.

Microsoft Research, in particular, has extended the concept of using monkeys to test mobile apps by creating monkeys to generate various responses to web requests that help expose flawed assumptions made by developers (that a web server will always respond without complaint).[43] By using these network monkeys, these flawed assumptions/implementations can be found quickly so that they can be fixed before the app is shipped, and the app can be made more robust and resilient. The developer may also be able to improve the user experience. For instance, they could include a GUI that enables users to log in to websites that require the user to log in before it will provide the contents.

3) SCALING TESTING

Scaling testing enables more testing to be done than we would be able to achieve ourselves. There are various approaches including: using remote

---

[41] Harty, J.: Test Automation Interfaces for Mobile Apps. LogiGEAR Magazine, 13 Dec 2012; logigear.com

[42] UI/Application Exerciser Monkey.

[43] Ravindranath, L., Nath, S., Padhye, J., Balakrishnan, H. "Automatic and Scalable Fault Detection for Mobile Applications." ACM, 2014.

devices, including other people in the testing, and running tests on device farms, often in parallel.

Distributed Testing

Testing does not have to be local to the development team. In fact, there are several approaches where the testing can be distributed. The first is to remotely access devices elsewhere in the world, often over a web-based connection, for instance to connect to a hosted device in another country. These may support interactive testing and/or remote execution of automated tests depending on what the hosting platform provides. The second approach is where the testing is delegated to people remotely who test using phones they have available. There are various crowd-sourced testing services available where organisations can arrange and pay for remote testing to be performed by trusted testers who are not employed directly by the organisation.

Device Farms

Device farms were first launched around 2007 with Nokia's Remote Device Access service and a commercial offering provided by Mobile Complete. Various companies also had internal, private device farms. Since then there has been a steady growth of device farms available for performing remote testing. These include services from Xamarin,[44] Testdroid,[45] and SauceLabs,[46] that changed the focus from hands-on remote testing to running automated tests on more devices in parallel. In 2015 both Amazon and Google launched internet-based test farms[47,48] that may help to make the services less expensive and more mainstream. Amazon even provides a basic automated test service called fuzz[49] as an option (although it appears to be more of a test monkey service).

---

[44] https://xamarin.com/test-cloud

[45] http://testdroid.com/

[46] https://saucelabs.com/

[47] https://aws.amazon.com/device-farm/

[48] https://developers.google.com/cloud-test-lab/?hl=en

[49] http://docs.aws.amazon.com/devicefarm/latest/developerguide/testtypes-built-in-fuzz.html

Microsoft uses farms of virtual devices to run vast numbers of fully automated exploratory tests for thousands of apps for their mobile platform. The virtual devices enable them to run these tests quickly and very inexpensively. Their tests seek generic bugs that affect the apps rather than bugs related to specific devices.[50]

Device farms can help scale your tests and provide you with access to a wider range of devices than you may have available locally. We predict there will be further acquisitions and developments so device farms can offer more comprehensive, integrated automated testing.[51]

4) STATIC ANALYSIS

Static analysis assesses designs and files rather than running or testing the code. It is a useful complement to all the other forms of testing and can catch problems at the source, rather than once the app has been released.

Design reviews are a static analysis technique and remain useful in finding flaws in mobile apps. Similarly, code reviews, performed by developers who understand the relevant mobile platforms, can catch many bugs before they reach the application's codebase.

Traditionally, when static analysis is applied to the software, static analysis assesses source code. However, for mobile apps, in particular, static analysis is also used to assess generated code. The generated code may need to be extracted and decrypted from the binary application code. The main focus

[50] Ravindranath, L., Nath, S., Padhye, J., Balakrishnan, H. Automatic and Scalable Fault Detection for Mobile Applications. ACM, 2014.

[51] As an example, in Summer 2015 Amazon acquired AppThwack (https://appthwack.com/).

seems to be malware detection, privacy, and other security-related aspects of the app, something to consider when there is low trust of the developers, external libraries, or the development process.

The mobile app may include third-party source code and/or libraries. Consider reviewing them as they will become an inherent part of the app with the same rights and privileges as the rest of the app. We don't want the third-party code to adversely affect the user experience or the qualities of the app. In October 2015, Apple removed several hundred apps that included a rogue third-party library that breached privacy and Apple policies.[52]

Facebook provides a free tool called fbinfer[53] which is available for iOS and Android. The development tools (known as SDKs) also include static analysis capabilities. These can often be automatically run after each code check-in to help detect potential flaws and provide feedback before the developer has moved on to something else.

LIMITATIONS OF THESE FOUR PROVEN WAYS

Each of these ways of improving testing helps in isolation, provided the results are used to actually amend and improve the app they help test. These ways can also be combined, and done well, they help to complement and multiply the benefits.

However, even when projects apply static analysis techniques and tools, and combine them with better interactive testing and brilliant test automation,

---

[52] "Developers need to be aware that when they install an SDK in their app, they're responsible for how it affects their users." From iOS Apps Caught Using Private APIs; sourcedna.com; 18 Oct 2015

[53] http://fbinfer.com/

where the testing has been scaled across people in various locations and where the automated tests run on globally distributed farms of devices, the testing will still miss some of what is relevant and useful. In particular, they don't assess how the app is used by the population of end users or how users perceive the app. These gaps mean the app is at risk of failing for end users in ways we are not able to predict and ultimately of being rejected and abandoned by many of the users we desire. Thankfully, new techniques are emerging to help us fill these gaps by using analytics.

UNDERSTANDING MOBILE ANALYTICS AND FEEDBACK

In its September 2015 Market Guide for Mobile App Analytics, Gartner analysts state, *"mobile app analytics tools collect and report on in-app data pertaining to the operation of the mobile app and the behavior of users within the app, as well as aggregate market data on apps across public app stores"*.[54]

This chapter includes several related topics. These are analytics in general (albeit several examples come from the mobile domain), mobile analytics, and an emerging topic of analysing feedback from users.

Developers would like an easy way to monitor the vital signs of their mobile app: *"A visualization tool such as those hospital monitoring devices with heart rate, blood pressure, etc., would help to gain a better understanding of an app's health and performance"*.[55] Mobile analytics can finally answer their request. It can be the real-time surveillance system that continuously monitors all vital signs. Here, heart rate, SpO2, blood pressure, and cholesterol ratio are user experience, performance, stability, and usability.

---

[54]   Wong, J., Haight, Cameron, Leow, Adrian: Market Guide for Mobile App Analytics; Gartner; 15 Sept 2015.

[55]   Joorabchi, M. E., Mesbah, A., and Kruchten, P.: Real Challenges in Mobile App Development; Empirical Software Engineering and Measurement, IEEE; Oct 2013.

Mobile analytics is like the SEO for mobile apps; however, it helps optimise the app and the user experience rather than search engine rankings. There are some general practices that can help the majority of apps; as you gain competence, you will find ways to also optimise your work and how you use mobile analytics.

Feedback is perhaps the closest means we have, without directly interviewing users, of getting their impressions on the user experience and their perceptions of an app. Companies have realised that users have a voice and they're willing to speak publicly about their experiences with mobile apps.

MOBILE ANALYTICS CAN IMPROVE MOBILE APPS

Mobile analytics provides additional data from virtually all of the active user base of a mobile app. Rather than relying solely on our own ideas, thoughts, and feelings, we now have data we can use and analyse to understand how the app is being used, where, when, and on what devices, etc. App stores have started to provide some of the information, including recommendations, such as to add translations. Nonetheless, they don't provide the depth or richness of information that can be obtained with mobile analytics.

The development team can seek confirmation of their earlier predictions and identify anomalies, for instance on the popularity, the navigation flows, time taken, etc. for various aspects of the app so they then have the opportunity to make informed decisions, based on the data they've obtained.

From a business perspective, organisations can use the analytics to guide the product development, even to the extent of creating new apps.

Mobile analytics can provide an "Early Warning System" of live/run-time issues. It may provide lower latency, in terms of getting relevant feedback than app store reviews, and it can also be used to cross-check and corroborate complaints from users.

Conceptual App Feedback Cycles

AN OVERVIEW OF ANALYTICS

This and the following section cover the general concepts of analytics. They help set the scene and context for mobile analytics.

According to Wikipedia, analytics is defined as "the discovery and communication of meaningful patterns in data".[56] Therefore, it's driven by data where we apply techniques to glean useful, relevant insights so we can improve upon things.

---

[56] "Analytics", Wikipedia.

Key Questions Addressed by Analytics

In Analytics At Work,[57] Davenport identified key questions addressed by analytics, where most organisations concentrate on the information aspects rather than seeking the insights that analytics can bring.

	Past	**Present**	**Future**
Information	**What's happened?** (Reporting)	**What's happening now?** (Alerts)	**What will happen?** (Forecasting)
Insight	**How and why did it happen?** (Factor analysis)	**What is the next best action?** (Recommendation)	**What's the best/worst that can happen?** (Modeling / Simulation)

Key Questions Addressed by Analytics, from Analytics At Work

In the confluence chapter we reconsider these questions as they may apply to using mobile analytics to help test mobile apps.

[57] Davenport, T., Harris, J., and Morison, R.: "Analytics at Work." Harvard Business Publishing, Boston, MA; ISBN 978-1-422-17769-3, 2010.

Tracking Three Key Aspects:
Business, Social, and Technology

There are three broad purposes for using analytics: business, social, and technological. Here are some examples of each aspect.

- Business (ways to measure and grow the business, for instance revenues, reach, and traffic volumes are commonly used). The business aspect concentrates on viability and achieving the organisation's objectives. Viability often includes financial aspects, particularly for commercial organisations.

- Social (ways users communicate about the app, what's happening in their lives, and through their use of the app). Social focuses on the human elements; how users perceive the software, whether they feel sufficiently strongly to try to influence others, positively or negatively; and even potentially their mood.

- Technological (how the software is performing on the various computers and devices, including reporting potential and actual problems). The technological aspects include the app and related systems, they can affect the costs, constrain growth, and lead to user dissatisfaction. They can include operational analytics, including deployment of updates and all the backend servers and services. While they're seldom in the limelight, they underpin everything else. And as many companies are discovering, flaws and problems in the technological aspects can really sting when failures occur.

Here is a possible mapping between various forms of analytics related to mobile apps and the three primary purposes of using analytics from the perspective of an organisation or team.

Forms of Analytics

Form	Technical	Business	Social
Software Development	Yes	Cost-effectiveness & competitiveness	No
Feedback Paths	Yes	Yes	Yes
Usage	Yes	Yes	No
Technical & Sensors	Yes	Useful for risk assessments	May affect perceived trust in terms of their privacy, etc.
Crash	Yes	Useful for risk assessments	May affect the perceived quality of the app.
App Store Feedback	Maybe	Yes	Yes

PROCESSING FEEDBACK

Here we discuss a related topic to mobile analytics, that of processing feedback, particularly feedback that's been provided on app stores. Other sources include social media websites, video websites, etc.

App Store Feedback

App stores provide a key source of feedback as they're a well-known rendezvous, influential, and relatively easy to mine in order to obtain usable data. App store feedback can include recommendations and requests from users worth considering and reports of problems that might otherwise go unnoticed by the development team. We will use examples for an Android app called Kiwix, one which Julian Harty co-develops and supports.

Reviews of Kiwix Android App

One of the first activities one can do is compare the ratings with the comments, as some common patterns may emerge. These patterns may unearth feature requests, including ones where the user offers to increase their rating once the feature has been implemented. The confluence chapter includes several worked examples of analysing feedback where we discovered several feature requests in the process.

If you would like to know more about working with feedback on apps, here are some useful resources.

- A very readable book on ways to improve app quality, including analysis of feedback in app stores, is *App Quality, Secrets of Agile App Teams* (ISBN 978-1-499-75127-7) by Jason Arbon.

- There are various interesting academic papers investigating app store ratings and reviews. Here are a couple well worth reading:

  - "Why People Hate Your App – Making Sense of User Feedback in a Mobile App Store" (http://chbrown.github.io/kdd-2013-usb/kdd/p1276.pdf).

  - "What Do Mobile App Users Complain About?" (http://dx.doi.org/10.1109/MS.2014.50). One of the key insights here is that, overall, 2-star reviews identify more serious issues than those reported in 1-star reviews.

Challenges Working with App Store Data

There are various challenges related to working with app store data, with regard to the feedback posted online about a particular app. These include the volume of feedback, where popular apps from Google and Facebook may receive several thousand items of feedback per day, spam and unethical feedback (including paid-for ratings to skew the overall rating), coping with multiple languages, and interpreting what people write. Some feedback may be misinterpreted. For instance, sentiment analysis can have problems correctly interpreting negatives, sarcasm, and slang.

A related consideration is realising that customers may have very different perceptions of "quality". According to the research on customer-perceived quality by Mockus et al:[58] "Some measures of customer perceived quality can vary by up to 30 times ... This indicates the profound importance ... in managing customer perceived quality, especially when a customer's expectations are high". The authors also discussed the impossibility of being able to replicate all the customer environments during system verification. The data may be hard to obtain and only available briefly, so it may need to be retrieved often and stored locally (while upholding privacy aspects of hosting personally identifiable information).

Inconsistent Feedback

Another challenge related to working with app store data is when feedback contains internal inconsistencies. For example, Kiwix received 5 stars even though links were broken in that release. These inconsistencies hint at some of the challenges of analysing user-provided feedback, especially automatically.

Ebrahim Salarvand August 28, 2015
★★★★★
Hi In Samsung Galaxy S3, links are not respond. Please fix it. Thanks.

Wikimedia CH August 17, 2015
Thank you for your feedback. This bug should be fixed now in the last version 1.96. May you please check it?

Inconsistent Feedback

58   Predictors of customer perceived software quality

We will now move on to two related topics: sentiment analytics and emotional analytics. Both can be usefully applied to analysing user-provided feedback. In addition, they offer the potential to gather passive information (where the user doesn't explicitly provide feedback) albeit with potential privacy implications.

Sentiment Analytics

Understanding what users think, or at least write, about our apps can help us find aspects worth improving in the app, and provide additional sources of testing ideas.

Sentiment analytics process a user's communication about the app to determine the emotions the user intends to communicate to other people. Satisfied and happy users may recommend and promote an app, while unhappy and dissatisfied users may try to dissuade people from using an app, business, or service. Organisations may need to be able to react quickly, appropriately, and positively in response to both positive and negative sentiments.

As users often use social media, app store feedback, and other online forums, their written communication is often easy to access and analyse. App store feedback was covered in more detail earlier in this chapter.

If you are interested in evaluating sentiment analysis, there are various freely available projects available, including an opensource Android app,[59] and LingPipe, which has a tutorial[60] on sentiment analysis. Be prepared to work directly with code as you will learn by doing. Another software project from Stanford[61] includes some interesting comments about the accuracy of the sentiment analysis in various circumstances.

---

[59] Tweentiment

[60] LingPipe tutorial

[61] http://nlp.stanford.edu/sentiment/code.html

There are numerous research papers, including two aptly named papers,"*How Do Users Like This Feature? A Fine Grained Sentiment Analysis of App Reviews,*" [62] and "*Why People Hate Your App – Making Sense of User Feedback in a Mobile App Store*".[63] Both these papers are well worth reading.

There's also an online book available, called *Opinion mining and sentiment analysis,*[64] that covers many of the core concepts.

Using Real User Sentiment Analysis to Improve Application Testing and Customer Support

Provided by:
Matt Johnson, *Chief Marketing Strategy Officer, Applause*

Here is a real-life example of how sentiment analysis helped improve the testing of a mobile app. They were similarly able to help improve customer support.

A leading U.S.-based retailer uses mobile sentiment analysis to measure and monitor how effectively their apps satisfy users' wishes. Beyond this voice of the customer (VOC) use case, however, this retailer has found two novel uses for this treasure trove of user sentiment data.

---

[62] https://mobis.informatik.uni-hamburg.de/wp-content/uploads/2014/06/FeatureSentiments.pdf

[63] http://chbrown.github.io/kdd-2013-usb/kdd/p1276.pdf

[64] Pang, B. and Lee, L.: Opinion mining and sentiment analysis; Cornell; 2008.

- User sentiment data is used to help define and refine the quality assurance investments that are made. This is done via a collaboration between a Business Intelligence (BI) team and the Quality Assurance (QA) team. QA departments tend to define their test coverage requirements (across use cases, devices, OSes, browsers, carriers, etc.) based on what they've done in the past. By bringing a BI mindset to defining what needs to be tested, this retailer has expanded testing efforts where they can make the greatest impact, and decreased them where they have the least effect on real-world users.

- User sentiment data is used to help improve product documentation and customer support. This same retailer is mining mobile user sentiment data to help identify and correct gaps in their product documentation – and in the training and materials used by their customer support team. By ensuring that assets (help documentation and trained support reps) are in place for the most common user issues – and keeping up with these changing patterns as an application evolves – this retailer is using real customer data to deliver greater customer delight.

Emotional Analytics

Software is now available that claims to measure a user's emotions, using visual[65] and auditory[66] sources of data. They provide their results within a few seconds, almost in real time. However, based on one of the author's tests, the results were not very accurate; nonetheless, these apps provide early indications of the concepts. Researchers are even able to detect boredom from mobile phone usage[67] by analysing data from devices over extended periods of days or more.

Some of these measurements involve collecting additional data that may not be appropriate for your application. However, it's also worth considering how relevant a user's emotions are in terms of them using your app and how relevant mood is in terms of testing the app.

APPLYING ANALYTICS

By themselves, analytics do little good. They need to be applied productively. In the industry there are three main ways they are applied – descriptively, predictively, and prescriptively. We will cover each briefly in turn.

---

[65] http://www.affectiva.com/solutions/mobile/

[66] http://www.beyondverbal.com/

[67] When Attention is not Scarce - Detecting Boredom from Mobile Phone Usage

Descriptive Analytics

Descriptive analytics are able to describe what has happened, thereby allowing us to gain insights such as the causes of how and why something happened. These insights may help us to improve our work in the future, for instance by avoiding similar problems. Most organisations use analytics for descriptive purposes.

Predictive Analytics

Predictive analytics can tell us what is likely to happen. Historical data is processed and machine learning provides the predictions. They do not predict what *will* happen, they predict what *may* happen. They may offer several alternatives.

We can then use the predictions to make decisions before the predictions take effect, for instance to increase capacity of servers in the cloud so that the system can cope with predicted increases in traffic volumes. They may conversely predict when the system may have spare capacity where we can schedule data processing on otherwise idle equipment, perform maintenance and upgrades, etc.

Eric Siegel's book *Predictive Analytics*[68] is an extremely readable introduction to the topic. And as Davenport identified, analytical insights can help predict aspects of the future.[69]

---

[68] Siegel, E.: Predictive Analytics. Wiley; ISBN 978-1-118-35685-2, 2013.

[69] Davenport, T., Harris, J., and Morison, R.: "Analytics at Work." Harvard Business Publishing, Boston, MA; ISBN 978-1-422-17769-3, 2010.

Prescriptive Analytics

One step beyond predictive analytics is where the analytics recommends an action. In the confluence chapter we discuss some of the risks associated with computers making recommendations. Nonetheless, prescriptive analytics can provide insights that can help us make informed decisions. As machine-learning improves, the prescriptions may include clear explanations that people can understand correctly so they can decide whether they disagree with any of the reasons why the software is prescribing a particular course or action.

ANALYTICS FOR MOBILE APPS

In the previous sections we provided the context for the rest of this chapter where we turn to the world of mobile apps. For the authors, mobile analytics refers to analytics incorporated into a mobile app, what could be described as in-app analytics. We will expand the context so you can learn about similar and complementary analytics.

An Overview of Mobile Analytics

The mobile app needs a way to report data about the device and what the app is doing. In most cases this involves adding a software library to the app, which does much of the hard work. However, some projects have written their own software to do similar stuff. The library may include an API, a way that the mobile app can provide additional information, which will be reported by the analytics library.

The data needs to be sent to servers which will collect, store, and process it. Most mobile apps use commercial analytics services where a company provides the service, including the servers, so the app development team can focus on the app, rather than the analytics infrastructure.

As you probably know, first-hand, internet connections are not always freely available so the mobile app's analytics library needs to cope with interruptions in network connectivity and only send the data when the connection is available.

The following figure provides an overview of how mobile analytics sends and processes the raw data.

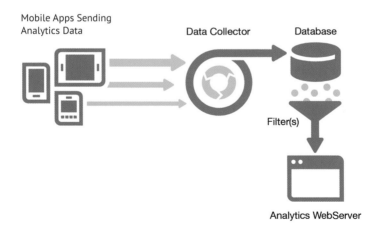

Overview of Mobile Analytics
(Each step may be delayed)

What is Special About Mobile Analytics?

There are several reasons why mobile analytics are special and distinct from other technologies such as traditional web analytics used by websites. Intriguingly, web apps, particularly when used on mobile devices, can borrow some of the design and architectural aspects of mobile analytics when they use local storage, and rich client-side processing, to provide functionality regardless of the current state of the internet connection.

The Library is a First-Class Citizen

Software libraries, when incorporated into a mobile app, have the same rights and privileges as the overall app. Libraries can use the same resources and access the same personal data as the app. If the app has access to the user's contacts, so does the library. By comparison, for web content, the libraries are distinct and separate – they are third-party software. They can be blocked by the user in their web browser, they have more restricted access to user data, and legislation such as the EU Cookie Law[70] applies. There is a helpful privacy guide[71] that directly discusses mobile analytics. It also describes various good practices your users may appreciate you following online, published by the Information Commissioner's Office in the UK.

---

[70] EU Cookie Law: A readable guide on the implications of the legislation is available at https://ico.org.uk/for-organisations/guide-to-pecr/cookiesand- similar-technologies/

[71] Privacy in mobile apps, Guidance for app developers; ico.org.uk; 2013.

Data Connections Aren't Guaranteed

For users of personal computers in static locations, the connection to the internet tends to be reliable and "always on". Web analytics and other software can assume the connection will be reliable and available. For mobile apps, particularly when the user is mobile, it would be unwise to assume the connection is available and reliable. There are many reasons why an app may not currently have a viable network connection, for instance if the device is in flight-mode, or when there is no network coverage currently. As most mobile analytics is designed to send the data using the internet, part of the design needs to consider how the library will behave when there is no viable internet connection. Some libraries discard the data, others may save and forward some, or all, of the interim data. It's important you know how the library is intended to behave and to test its behaviour so you know what it actually does in the circumstances.

What to Measure in a Mobile App

Mobile apps include screens in the GUI, events and actions within the UI, and business-specific events and actions. To measure these, the mobile analytics library needs to provide appropriate features and capabilities. There are also device-specific details, such as the model, operating system version, available resources, and how hard the device is working, which may be relevant and useful. Again, the library needs to be able to collect and send the relevant data.

Differences from Web Analytics

Forrester found that nearly half of companies that use mobile analytics to deliver their mobile analytics trends use ones originally designed for websites.[72] Analytics designed for the web does not reflect various aspects of a mobile app, such as services, transactions, or the run-time environment. Also, the libraries may not cope well when a connection is not available. Will they store events and forward them when the network is next available?

Analytics Throughout the Mobile App Ecosystem

There is more to mobile analytics than mobile analytics! Here we briefly cover various sources of analytics in the overall ecosystem.

- Software Development Analytics focuses on the software development (and testing) aspects of our work, as we use computers and software inherently when working on mobile apps. There are rich veins of data about what we are doing, including: the bugs that are found, time to investigate and triage, time to fix, effectiveness of the testing, latency of the testing, etc.

- Analytics about how the app is being used (usage.)

- Analytics about the conditions the app is being used in both within the device – e.g., available memory, CPU load, sensor values – and beyond the device – e.g., network characteristics, responses from remote servers, etc. (technical and sensors.)

---

[72] Use Analytics To Create Mobile Best Practices, Forrester, May 2015.

- Analytics of detected failures (crash-analytics.)

- Analytics of processing user-provided feedback (e.g., processing of app store feedback.)

Finally for this section, as we start to apply analytics, we can use analytics to gain insights into the effectiveness and value of how we are using the other analytics.

This meta-analytics can help inform us about the value of feedback paths and what we do with the data received through specific feedback paths. One way to measure the value is the concept of signal-to-noise ratio of each feedback path. Another relevant measure is the latency – how long it takes for information to flow through the particular path, and then how long it takes us to act on the information when we have received it.

Software Development Analytics

Microsoft Research has been investigating how to apply analytics to improve software development, as software development is a data-rich environment awash with data about development, bugs, automated tests, and lots more. A good introduction is one of their papers,[73] where they modified Davenport's matrix to apply it to software development. Another research project, called SAMOA,[74] provides visual analytics specifically for mobile apps. They discovered mobile apps have specific development characteristics, for instance minimal use of inheritance in the codebase. Subsequent work discovered that code tends to have more bugs when it uses platform-specific dependencies. As

[73] Buse, R. P. L. and Zimmermann, T.: Analytics for Software Development. 2010

[74] A readable introduction to the SAMOA project including the goals and rationale is available online: Minelli, R.: Software Analytics for Mobile Applications. Master's Thesis; June 2012.

the authors of the research say, "platform dependence may be used to prioritize the most defect-prone source code for code reviews and unit testing by the software quality assurance team".[75]

Causes of Mobile Analytics

There are two main causes, or triggers, for mobile analytics. They are broadly user-centric or app-centric triggers.

Event-Based Causes (App-Centric)

Event-based causes include transitions in the app's lifecycle at run-time, for instance when an app is started, paused, or killed. Timers, network requests and responses, device-wide broadcasts, etc. can also be considered events which may be relevant in terms of mobile analytics.

User Interaction-Based Causes (User-Centric)

User interactions are inherently related to the user, and therefore we may wish to collect analytics related to these user-centric actions and interactions. Examples of user-centric analytics include:

- GUI inputs (gestures, touches, text input)

- heatmaps (these will be covered shortly)

- haptics

- audio

- visual

---

75 Syer, M. Nagappan, M. Adams, B. and Hassan, A. E.: Studying the Relationship Between Source Code Quality and Mobile Platform Dependence; 2014

Complementary Analytics, Techniques, and Tools

Various software tools can provide different perspectives on the behaviour of a mobile app or how it is being used in practice.

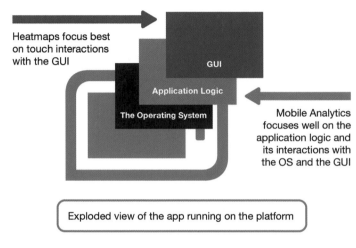

Layers of an App

- Heatmaps collect data on interactions between users and the GUI. There are at least ten vendors offering competing products. We will mention some interesting examples here and Philippe Dumont, the CEO of Azetone, has provided his perspective on using heatmaps for mobile apps.

- Profiling involves instrumenting an app to collect detailed run-time information of the inner workings of the software. For practical reasons this is done on a local device rather than in the field. Profiling can help identify potential performance issues either with specific parts of the software or on particular devices or operating system versions.

- Virtual networks enable the development team to reproduce various network conditions so they can test their impact and effects on software, and in our case on mobile apps that use the network. Hewlett Packard Enterprise offers their Network Virtualization[76] product, which has sophisticated algorithms to provide quite accurate reproduction of realistic network behaviours. There are various free offerings, including those provided with development tools for most of the major mobile platforms.

- Injecting faults into an environment can help expose flaws in how mobile apps cope and behave. Several people, including Microsoft Research in particular, have established ways to inject legitimate fault conditions, such as HTTP response error codes, to determine how mobile apps cope and behave. Sadly, they discovered many apps were not designed to handle these legitimate, and realistic, responses and some even crashed.

Analytics, such as heatmaps, record inputs such as touches and gestures which are inherently GUI orientated. These can be described as "touch-streams". GUI-based data capture can capture significantly more data, and potentially much more frequently, than those reported by basic mobile analytics. They may be reported similarly to the way mobile analytics events are sent. Appsee provide some useful e-books on visual analytics.[77]

---

[76] https://www8.hp.com/us/en/software-solutions/network-virtualization/

[77] https://www.appsee.com/ebooks

A Perspective on Heatmaps

This section is contributed by Philippe Dumont, CEO and founder of Azetone.[v]

Heatmaps track and aggregate all touch gestures into visual heatmaps. They can help answer the following questions.

- Which areas of each screen do users use the most?

- Which features are used and which should be changed or removed?

- Which UI elements are being ignored?

Delivering an outstanding Mobile User Experience (a.k.a. UX) is arguably the #1 Key Success Factor to achieve the best retention, engagement, and conversion rates with your app. But if you want to get a comprehensive view of user behaviour and interactions with your app, you will need to go beyond the traditional analytics solutions. Why? Because app analytics focus on providing you with data on the *"what"* (What are the typical user paths? What is the performance of the app like? What is the data on customer retention?) rather than the *"how"* (How do users really interact with your app and its user interface? How do you assess their user experience?).

---

[v]   http://azetone.com/

Mobile UX is a tricky subject. It differs from app performance or stability, it is harder to measure, and you may often not even realize that your app has some major UX flaws! These will not necessarily surface in negative app ratings (Hey, your App doesn't crash after all!) or result in angry customer feedback (Who would really bother writing up something about this?). They will just translate into limited app usage, high user drop-off rates, and disappointing app monetization.

To address these issues, there is a new generation of tools called Mobile Heatmaps or Mobile UX Analytics. These tools allow you to obtain insights into how users respond to your app design and UI and how to improve their overall user experience.

Why is this really important for your mobile app? Well, unlike a traditional website where you have full control and decision-making power when designing the user experience, a mobile app UX is subject to various external constraints. App stores dictate UI guidelines which become the de facto standard for apps as soon as they are released.

Your app will be compared with many other apps, including those of your competitors, and the apps your users most often use (for instance, Facebook, Yahoo Weather, or Airbnb).

Your users are constantly out there rating your app in public. You can't really afford a poor UX unless you are willing to take the risk of lower app reviews and therefore lower organic user acquisition rates.

To keep your app in the race and stand out from the crowd, you need to take control of your mobile user experience, and this is where mobile heatmaps can be of great help.

Understand How Your Mobile App is Being Used with Mobile Heatmaps

Mobile heatmaps are designed to provide a comprehensive mapping of all the gestures performed by users in your app. This is done by enabling a "finger tracking" feature in every screen of your app. It will record every touch on the screen, its type, and position. Heatmap analytics will process every tap, swipe, zoom, pinch, etc., and map them as an overlay on top of each screen of your app.

Example of a Heatmap

By analysing the reports, you will discover useful insights about your app usage and how to improve the user experience.

- For instance, you will be able to visualise whether some users are trying to interact with parts of your UI which are completely static.

- By analysing the time between two gestures on a given screen, you may surface some difficulties or hesitations in completing a task.

- By realising that users are scrolling a lot up and down your screens, you may realise that they might be looking for a next step that just seemed obvious to you.

Advanced Heatmap solutions enable you to collect and compare different heatmaps based on various criteria. If they are based on device information, you will be able to find out user behaviour based on type of smartphone, screen size or version of OS. If they include customer data, you will be able to surface differences of app usage between new and recurrent users, free and paying customers, or any other relevant user dimensions.

The additional information will help you target precisely where and for whom you may want to improve the user experience for your app.

**Examples of How Heatmaps
Can Help Improve the UX**

If a lot of taps are recorded just around an active touch zone,
your button is probably just too small or not well positioned.
If you have several important elements below the fold
(especially on certain devices) but your page is rarely scrolled
on those screens, your users are missing out and you should
probably reorganise your page design.

Alternatively, in the heatmap example, we can see many
users trying to zoom on the bag. However, the picture is not
an active touch zone and cannot be expanded, resulting in
a disappointing user experience. This learning can be easily
captured using heatmaps.

Multimodal Communications

In the figure App in Context we can see the app in the context of the overall
device with the main inputs and outputs. These physical inputs and outputs
map to several of our senses – sight, touch, and hearing – together with our
mediums of communication – touch, audio, and, indirectly, vision – where the
device and the app can use one or more of the cameras to (a) "see" the user or
(b) "see" what the user sees.

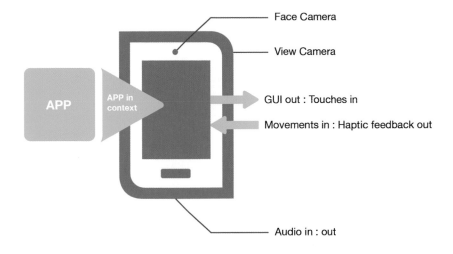

App in Context

As an example of one form of mobile analytics, heatmaps record touch inputs (or touch interactions, gestures, etc.) overlaid on visual outputs (what the app displays on the screen). It's also possible, of course, to record the software to software (or machine to machine) interactions. These interactions include network communications, File IO,[78] and system messages. Software events (such as timers firing) may also be relevant. Similarly, behaviour within the app, particularly "Exceptions" can, and often are, recorded.

---

[78] File IO is common shorthand for interactions between apps and various computer files. The files read by the app are inputs and those written are outputs. Some files are both read and written.

Why Does Our Welcome Page Have Such a High Quit Rate?
Zahi Boussiba, CEO and Co-Founder, Appsee

A mobile app company faced a very serious issue. One in three users were abandoning the app during the sign-up process. The users had to accept the Terms and Conditions by ticking an "I agree" checkbox, then tap the "agree and continue" button.

The company discovered the impediments after analysing their app's sign-up screen using Appsee's heatmap analytics.

Appsee Screen Heatmaps for the Problematic Screen

- The first issue was related to the flow: users were trying to fast-track the process by tapping the "agree and continue" button at the bottom of the screen. Users were stuck with an unresponsive button, thought the app was buggy, and left the app.

- The second one was related to the design: The "I agree" checkbox was too small to be interacted with and frustration led users to quit the app.

The mobile development team resolved the issue by enlarging the checkbox. They also added a simple notification to advise users to tick the checkbox if they pressed the "agree and continue" button before ticking the checkbox.

These 2 very minor changes helped increase the conversion by almost 27%.

Recording Progress

There are various ways progress can be recorded. At the most detailed level, all significant IOs (Inputs and Outputs) can be captured and reported under relevant circumstances. Appsee,[79] for instance, creates "video" recording (which seem more like frequent screenshots at 1 Hz) and transmits these, together with the touch-stream, when crashes occur. The recordings are likely to be limited to a subset of devices, by using sampling techniques to reduce the impact on users and the network.

---

[79] https://www.appsee.com/

Screenshots are quite detailed and may consume significant bandwidth. Mobile analytics libraries, such as AppPulse Mobile, generate and send an event on each screen transition. It may be possible and practical to match, or pair, these with a visual representation of each of the screens to approximate the GUI flows displayed, and presumably seen, by the user. Much less data needs to be transmitted for an event-based recording. However, some fidelity is lost, particularly how the UI is presented (the layout) on particular devices. And similarly, the details of the touch-stream aren't recorded so they aren't available for analysis.

The screens may extend beyond input forms, etc.; for instance, they may include maps, games, emails, videos, etc. In some cases, for example, maps, the coordinates, zoom, and other mapping settings could be captured and provided to enable the GUI to be reproduced for analysis.

Similarly, other forms of inputs and outputs could be captured and sent for analysis, for instance pictures of a person's face, recordings of their voice (and other sounds), etc. Settings, configurations, and their changes may also be relevant and germane to analysis.

For Now We See Through a Glass, Darkly...[80]

None of the various techniques capture or provide "everything". They are based on recording "some" and perhaps "enough" information to be useful. Later on we will cover some of the problems and risks of gathering too much information. For now, we'll assume we're trying to establish how much information is enough to be useful.

---

[80] Taken from Corinthians 13:12; https://www.biblegateway.com/passage/?search=1%20Corinthians%20 13:11-13&version=KJ21

One of the reasons why "everything" won't be available is that the behaviour of an app is seldom purely a factor of touch gestures on the GUI; often, there are several factors which (in combination) generate the resulting behaviour. Some factors are likely to be more relevant than others. However, the relevance of particular factors may vary from one aspect of the app to another. For instance, would background light be relevant for a face recognition algorithm used in an unlock screen app used on various Android apps? If so, how does the relevance vary? What about network conditions, other sensor inputs, etc.?

By analogy, we are able to recognise objects even when they're not as high a quality as we might wish or prefer. The example of increasing the resolution of an image containing the letter "R" shown in this figure taken from Wikipedia may be a useful illustration – we can start to recognise the letter once the resolution reaches 10x10, it's clearer at 20x20, and easy to discern at 50x50 pixels.

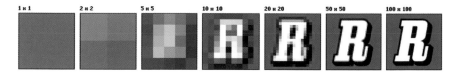

Resolution Illustration[81]

Similarly, we may be able to glean useful information using mobile analytics once a certain minimum resolution has been reached. In this case, resolution may be a factor of the types, frequency, and details contained in the various discrete messages sent by the mobile analytics libraries.

---

[81] "Resolution illustration". Licensed under Public Domain via Commons -
     https://commons.wikimedia.org/wiki/File:Resolution_illustration.png# /media/File:Resolution_illustration.png

Even seemingly basic information may help us improve our testing; for instance, the device model and available resources (CPU, storage, RAM, etc.) can help us decide which devices to test on. The device's locale can help us decide which languages to test the UI in, etc.

We're unlikely to obtain all the information needed to reproduce situations, contexts of use, etc. despite any claims to the contrary. Instead, we can decide on what information would be most relevant and useful, and then determine how well and how completely a particular mobile analytics library supports these requirements. We'll go into more detail later on about testing and selecting mobile analytics libraries.

Once we start receiving results from mobile analytics, we can use a technique called interpolation, "filling in the gaps or blanks" to connect events in order to establish sufficiently useful and realistic materials we can use for future testing of the app.

Gaps in the Data

There are inherently gaps in the data, where some details are not recorded. This holds for any inputs and outputs of the app and device. As we will discover, the answer is not simply to demand and gather more data more frequently; rather, the skill is to find ways to both fill the gaps and connect individual events into a related set of events that "tell a story" about what was happening. These stories can include user "journeys" as they are using the app, or working out causality where one event or action led to another which led eventually to something sufficiently important (such as a serious crash) where we want to know what happened.

What happens in the gaps may be relevant from an analysis and testing perspective. One of our challenges is to determine the relevance of data that's been recorded (some of it may *not* be relevant) and what is relevant from the data that has not been recorded or is not available. We need to ask and understand whether what happens in the gaps matters, e.g., the values, the interactions performed by the user, the run-time conditions and context, etc.

Determining Relevance of Inputs and Events

From a testing perspective as well as from performance-efficiency and user-privacy perspectives, it's important to determine the relevance of inputs and events and the sufficiency: how much information is *just enough* to enable us to materially improve our work and the end product, incorporating the app. It's wise and healthy to avoid collecting significantly more, or excessive, amounts of information. Ask yourself (and the project sponsors) the following:

- What do we need in the contents of events to enable us to understand what's germane?

- What are the effects of what we don't know or see?

- When do the details matter? Under what circumstances or conditions?

- How well and how accurately, do we need to reproduce the missing information?

- What and how do we need to safeguard the data?

- How could we make do with less information?

- How can we design tests that determine and exercise the variety of contexts, situations, and inputs the app (and user) need(s) to cope with?

One of the key skills and success factors of our work will be being able to determine the relevance of the many potential details that could affect the use of the app and its behaviours. We also need to be able to determine and decide the:

- Relevance, or irrelevance of details.

- Whether there is a coincidence, a correlation, or causation between the inputs (and context, etc.) and exposed flaws in the app.

COMPLEMENTARY DATA

Although we focus on mobile analytics, and it's a very rich source of information, it's useful to use complementary sources of data to cross-check data you obtain from mobile analytics. These sources can provide enough basic information to help you improve your testing locally, even without using mobile analytics.

Crash Reports

Crash reports capture and forward technical information about crashes that happened in your mobile app. They can be forwarded using a library that's integrated into the app (similar to the integration of mobile analytics, but typically simpler and with a tiny footprint in comparison), or the app store provider may automatically capture the crashes as part of their service.

We need to be able to understand what could have caused the crash – either our app didn't provide something that was expected by the code that crashed or our code wasn't designed to cope with a response it received. There are a couple of ways to do this. One way is to look at the source code of the app and work backwards to the possible inputs. Similarly, we may identify flaws in how the code handles the full set of responses, including malformatted ones and/or timeouts, etc. Another possible approach uses a concept called breadcrumbs (where developers preemptively add code to record a trace of what is happening). Yet another approach is where the app incorporates a recording of what happened before. Through these approaches we may be have enough clues to understand and possibly reproduce the crash so the development team can then modify the code so the app provides the correct inputs and is able to cope with the full set of responses.

Log Files

Log files are used by all the main mobile operating systems, and virtually all apps write messages to the log file. These messages often contain useful clues on what's happening and when problems occur. Log files are easy to access if you have direct access to the device; otherwise, they are private unless your app has permission to access them. In practice, they're useful for local analysis and debugging on local devices. There may be privacy issues reading them from user's devices.

The data in the log files can be filtered to remove irrelevant entries, e.g., from unrelated apps, and to reduce the volume of data to analyse. Mobile platforms (such as Android and iOS) automatically record errors that occur in apps in addition to messages reported by the various apps, so there may be enough clues (similar to those provided when using application-generated breadcrumbs) to work out possible causes for problems. In a similar way to using mobile analytics events, log messages can provide an indication of how the app is being used, which may be useful for testing and analysis.

Log data from mobile devices is seldom used as a source for analytics as they are private to the device and there may be significant privacy and other legal implications of "mining" the log data, particularly where the data is from other apps.

Comparing Log Messages and Analytics Events

The following figure presents a couple of the main informational outputs of an app: log messages and analytics events.

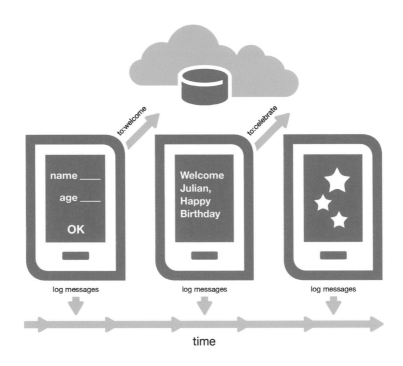

Examples of Recording Information

Analytics messages are externally oriented (they will be sent away for analysis and reporting). They communicate something of what the user is doing, or what's happening oriented around the user or the app. Their contents tend to be at a higher level than log messages, aimed at answering "what is the app doing?".

Log messages are internally oriented, relatively short lived (they are automatically overwritten as more log messages arrive), detail oriented, and intended to primarily help the developer understand what their code is doing.

They may include an indicator of importance or severity of the message. They are intended to remain on the device, rather than being exported; however, apps can request permission to read the log on Android, and there is a similar way for iOS apps to read the system logs.[82]

Neither log messages nor analytics events are intended to provide every detail; instead, they report what's deemed key at that point in the running code. Their format and properties are consistent for that point in the code; however, the values may change from one message to the next based on the run-time conditions and inputs to the app.

Profiling

Profiling is a technique used by developers where the code is modified to record, in detail, how the code is running. Often it includes timing information and is therefore used particularly to identify areas where the performance of the code is poor. Developers can then tune the code to improve the performance.

Like log data, profiling is developer oriented and seldom collected from user's devices.

SUMMARY OF MOBILE ANALYTICS

We have covered many topics related to what mobile analytics is and some of the ways it can be useful independently of software testing. Now it's time to move on to the next topic: how mobile analytics can help improve testing of mobile apps.

---

[82] Here are examples of an article (https://www.cocoanetics.com/2011/ 03/accessing-the-ios-system-log/) and an opensource project (https:// github.com/billgarrison/SOLogger) for accessing iOS logs.

CONFLUENCE BETWEEN MOBILE ANALYTICS AND SOFTWARE TESTING

" Connect the tester with the customer...using data. "
– Alan Page, Microsoft.[83]

INTRODUCTION

Mobile testing and mobile analytics are both independently valuable. However, the value increases significantly when they are combined effectively. The confluence represents the "coming together" of the two topics. Mobile analytics can help improve the testing. Also, testing the mobile analytics can help improve how it works and reduce the likelihood that the mobile analytics will produce undesirable and/or erroneous results.

Applying mobile analytics to improve testing is an emerging topic, one that's likely to rank as one of the most capable and powerful approaches to improve testing as the field becomes more established. As the "Feedback Cycles" figure indicates, mobile analytics can also complement other sources of feedback, including test

---

[83] Page, A.: "The Mobile Application Compatibility Challenge," Mobile Deep Dive conference, 06 Nov 2015.

results, feedback from users, and crash analytics. Later in this chapter we provide examples of how user-provided feedback can also help improve testing of mobile apps.

The two sources (mobile analytics and user feedback) can complement each other to help improve our testing. They take different paths, and reflect different perspectives. Mobile analytics only records what the instrumented app has been configured to provide; users don't need to do anything specific to provide the data – the data records aspects of what the app is doing, and reflects how the app is being used. Feedback from users is initiated by them and they choose what to say, and how and where to say it. The data may contain fresh insights and ideas that the app developers haven't considered before.

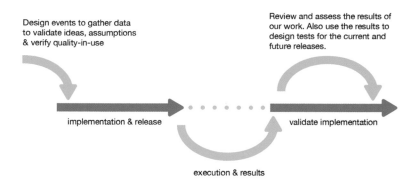

Design events to gather data to validate ideas, assumptions & verify quality-in-use

Review and assess the results of our work. Also use the results to design tests for the current and future releases.

implementation & release

validate implementation

execution & results

Feedback Cycles between Testing and Mobile Analytics for the App

Before we dive into the details, let's briefly consider the value of combining mobile analytics and testing from three perspectives: the business, the end users, and in terms of testing the apps.

Value to Business

For the business, the confluence can reduce the cost and latency in getting apps and updates to the market. They also reduce the risk of adverse problems in production, and enable testers to be engaged sooner if things are going awry in production. Decisions can be made based on rich, live data, rather than being limited to what the team thinks and is capable of.

Value to Users

For end users, they are likely to get higher-quality apps. In return, they "pay" in terms of the costs of the data traffic and by providing background information when the app is being used. Users are likely to appreciate the higher quality and therefore (a) use the app more, and for longer, and (b) rate the app positively and recommend it to more potential users.

Value to Testing

For testers, they have rich veins of additional data they can use to guide their work and the testing they do. They may be able to reduce low-value and low-grade work. Also, their work can be more rewarding as they can see the effects of the results of their work in a near real-time, ongoing basis. We will go into more detail in the next section.

Value of the Confluence for Testing and Testers

Inherently mobile analytics data provides access to insights into the app's behaviour in the wild. We can use the information to create tests based on realistic examples of how the app is being used by end users. Applying the information helps reduces guesswork in the tests we design and execute. Mobile analytics can capture performance data, both for individual actions and for overall processes such as registering an account. The data can help calibrate and corroborate mobile performance test results.

The figure Analytics for Testing of Mobile Apps refines the questions raised by Davenport[84] (and reproduced in the section Key Questions Addressed by Analytics) so we can identify ways mobile analytics can inform the testing of the respective mobile app.

	Past	Present	Future
Information (What, implicitly when, & perhaps where & who?)	**Was our testing on-target?**	**What should we test now?**	**What should we test next?**
Insight (How? Why?)	**What were the reasons why gaps occurred?**	**Justification and value for doing the current testing.**	**Designing and refining what data to collect using mobile analytics.**

Analytics for Testing of Mobile Apps

Mobile analytics may help us to test more smartly; for instance, the data may make some of our previous tests redundant, where equivalent data is available online. We may also be able to identify low-priority or low-value tests, for instance, of features that aren't really being used.

We can also use our testing skills to help design appropriate measures to be implemented using mobile analytics. Once these are implemented and incorporated into the app, we will start to collect information that can help validate our quality-in-use requirements, and gather feedback on the effectiveness of the tests we did and didn't do for that release. Ideally, there won't be any crashes or flaws reported if our testing was "fit-for-purpose" (assuming any related issues were fixed prior to release). Furthermore, as we gather data from mobile analytics, we can then design better tests for future releases of the app.

[84] Davenport, T., Harris, J., and Morison, R.: "Analytics at Work." Harvard Business Publishing, Boston, MA; ISBN 978-1-422-17769-3, 2010.

EXAMPLES OF HOW USING MOBILE ANALYTICS CAN HELP USERS AND THE BUSINESS

One of our goals is to help remove impediments that cause users to stop using the mobile app. Impediments can include problems installing the app on their device, confusion, or a lacklustre experience when they first try using the app. Analytical insights into how new users navigate through the app, and where they seem to flounder or abandon aspects of the app, can help us to design tests based on these user experiences.

Usability testing techniques, including interviews, can be based on live data from the field. Furthermore, we can prioritise finding, addressing, and fixing bugs and significant flaws, particularly in the commonly used areas of the apps that people initially encounter.

EXAMPLES OF HOW MOBILE ANALYTICS HELPS WITH TESTING

Here are various examples of how mobile analytics can help improve the testing of mobile apps.

- A tester discovered a large group of users of the app were in Paris, using the app in French. The team had enough information to change the types of tests and include testing the app in French. Similarly, you may discover regions where your apps are popular and model your testing to increase the chances of satisfying these users with future releases of your app.

- We can discover more about the power consumption while an app is running on various devices and find ways to improve the behaviour of our app. Battery drain varied by a factor of three for similar hardware specifications.[85] The developers were able to reduce battery drain by 40% for the Kindle Fire by reducing screen brightness when the app was running. As a result, the session lengths increased significantly on these devices. Users tend to use apps for longer when the apps use less power.

- We can model usage based on different network connections. Users preferred Wi-Fi and used apps more when they are connected with Wi-Fi. Conversely, higher network latencies reduced interaction by 40%.[85] Knowing these details can help us make sure we test under more realistic conditions and focus on tuning how the app uses the network so that we optimise it to keep the latencies low even on slower network connections.

- We can obtain detailed data on how the app is being used on various current and new devices. Research[85] found there was twice the usage of an app on tablets than smartphones. We can adapt our testing to reflect the usage on various devices, for instance, by performing some longer-running tests to reflect how users use the app. We may also detect anomalies where the usage on particular devices (such as the Kindle Fire example earlier) doesn't fit the trend compared to seemingly similar devices. We can then focus our analysis and testing on the devices where anomalies occur as we may discover and be able to fix problems that reduce the usage. Conversely, we may find ways to increase and extend usage from understanding the performance characteristics of devices where usage is above average. Another way mobile analytics can help is by providing early evidence of the app being used on new devices, perhaps ones we've not even heard of until now.

- We can protect and potentially enhance revenue through new releases of an app. A project discovered returning users provided over twice the revenue of new users, and when the app was updated to appeal to new users, they realised there was greater value in focusing on returning users and maintaining a continuity of features that those users value.[85]

---

[85]   "Capturing Mobile Experience in the Wild: A Tale of Two Apps."

- Our tests can become more relevant, based on evidence and reducing the need for guesswork. Mobile analytics identifies usage patterns, user journeys, etc. of the app so we can reflect usage more accurately in our tests. Mobile analytics can also make usage easier to reproduce, and may make crashes easier to identify, understand, and therefore fix.

OPTIMISE YOUR TESTING

There are many ways mobile analytics can help optimise aspects of your testing. These include:

- Selecting the devices to test the app on.

- Creating tests based on mobile analytics (various examples throughout this chapter) and user feedback.

- Prioritising the tests to run, and when to run them. This topic is introduced in the Test Recommendation Engine section.

Selecting Devices

There are a multitude of distinct mobile devices, and as many of us know, apps can behave very differently on different models. So it may be prudent to test on more than one device model. Some teams simply use a subset of the devices they have accumulated, while others select devices based on popularity of the device or of their app on those devices.

Recent research[86] discovered a better strategy for Android apps: tests are run on the devices where users write most of the reviews, thereby increasing the

---

perceived quality of the app as improving. The app for these devices is more likely to increase the app store ratings. Also, the reviews can help pinpoint problematic devices so teams can focus their testing and bug fixing to make the app work better on these devices (leading to better customer satisfaction and, hopefully, better ratings). TestDroid[87] also discovered some devices are more likely to be problematic (or expose more bugs depending on how you look at it).

When considering how to select devices, for Android, at least, using a mix of devices with different operating system versions is more important than covering other device characteristics when using a "practical" number of devices, around 4 or 5.[88]

How Many? Diminishing Returns

There is a tradeoff between the number of devices on which we test an app compared to the cost and time taken to do so. Furthermore, unless we have a honed, effective method of selecting additional devices that increase the variations, we may simply be wasting our resources. We recommend you gather data on which bugs are reported on various devices and which bugs you find subsequently during your testing on particular devices so that as you continue to test, you can create your own model to decide how many devices are sufficient.

You may also be able to decide the priority order for your testing, for instance smoke testing on one of your faster, more capable devices (so you get speedy feedback of any major issues), followed by testing on the most popular relevant devices, and finally some of the additional devices to maximise the diversity.

---

[87] Testdroid: Automated Remote UI testing on Android

[88] Vilkomir, S., Marszalkowski, K., Perry, C., and Mahendrakar, S.: "Effectiveness of Multi-device Testing Mobile Applications." 2nd ACM International Conference on Mobile Software Engineering and Systems, 2015.

Using Virtual Devices

Virtual devices seldom have the fidelity to be high-fidelity substitutes for physical devices in terms of performance, sensors, or – of course – device-specific flaws or bugs. However, they are very useful when they complement physical devices, and when we want to focus on general flaws that may affect an app or the underlying codebase. Later in the book, in the Test Monkeys section, we provided some examples of how Microsoft Research used automated test monkeys, which were run on a large array of virtual devices. By doing so they were able to reduce costs and scale the testing massively, compared to testing on physical devices.

Virtual devices can also help test facets not yet available to you (for instance a custom screen resolution) or where you'd like to easily fake some of the sensor values (for instance for the GPS) and when there are new releases of the operating system not yet available for use on devices.

An Epiphany

Yan Auerbach, Co-founder and COO Speechtrans Inc.

I had an epiphany when a friend of mine raised $1,000,000 USD funding. In his words: *"I just showed the investors the Analytics which explained that our app was being used more than the calendar app which was pre-loaded on their device, and that was all they needed to see it was a binary decision to invest or not invest, and based on the analytics it pointed to their decision to invest".* I had become laser focused on utilising analytics within our own app since it was not something we have done in the past other than as an afterthought. I became

---

obsessed with analytics and wanted to be able to understand our customers better than they knew themselves. My co-founder had told me for years to add a Currency Converter in our translation app, but I fought back stating it's not our core competency. As it turns out, our currency converter is the third most utilized function of our app now.

Prior to AppPulse Mobile there was a constant conflict with my programmers. Each time I would tell them to add analytics, they refused because it would slow their primary job, which was development of the app, and for four years it didn't happen. They claimed that as we have 44 language pairs, the implementation would require several thousand lines of code to properly log which language pair was selected the most often, and by which device, and how well it worked, etc.

It was not until I was in Barcelona at HP Discover in 2014 when I heard a magic word called "tagless" which changed the way that I thought about software development moving forward. I ended up meeting the reps of AppPulse Mobile. From what I saw I thought it was possibly the silver bullet for analytics for mobile apps, however I wanted to see for myself because I believe if something sounds too good to be true, it typically is.

I managed to sign up for the beta program and within 15 minutes, I had our app instrumented using this tool. I started collecting analytics like I never imagined possible. Within the first 24 hours I discovered our end users were spending 44 seconds on the registration screen. I immediately instructed my developers to stop all the work that they were doing and focus solely on adding single sign on to the registration page. The next day we released an update that got us 5-star reviews in the app stores and brought the registration time down to 7 seconds. Without the analytics tools we might have continued for 4 more years without understanding that it's not what we want to add to our software that's important. **It's what the end users want.**

The tagless approach means we don't need to write code to generate the mobile analytics data. As a small team this made a tremendous difference. Prior to learning about this tool we estimated we would require a dedicated developer to maintain the analytics module within the application and generate reports.

MOBILE ANALYTICS AS THE SPICE TO HPE'S SUGGESTED TEST PLAN

Before HP split into two independent organisations they published a proposed test plan for mobile apps. Their test plan helps illuminate various relevant topics. Therefore, the test plan forms the basis for the rest of this section. We will consider how mobile analytics might relate to each of these topics.

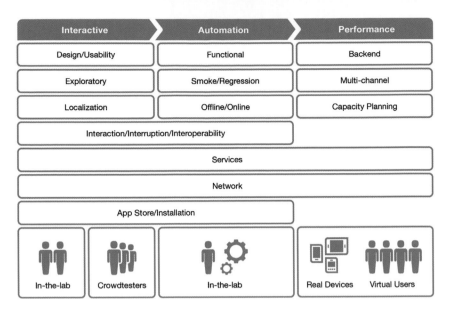

Optimise Your Test Plan

We'll identify primary and secondary sources where we believe particular mobile analytics tools are relevant.

Design

In-app mobile analytics may not help directly in terms of the GUI. Instead, good sources of analytics include sentiment and social analytics to help designers improve the design of the GUI. Mobile analytics provides data on usage, which can help inform designers of the effects of their designs.

Usability

Mobile analytics helps identify funnels for processes supported by the app (e.g., placing an order), and establish user flows and popularity of various aspects of the app, etc. It can also help record aspects of learnability and task completion (including where the task is completed correctly).

Mobile analytics can help detect where users are confused, e.g., where they seem to loop without making progress, where they stall, where they bypass things we consider relevant/useful/helpful/germane, etc.

The primary source is in-app analytics; various other forms of analytics, including social and sentiment analysis help us to interpret and obtain insights from what the end users are saying about their perceptions of the usability of the app. The *App Quality* book contains an interesting chapter on gleaning usability-related feedback from reviews on app stores.

Functional

Mobile analytics helps capture that users are able to complete various functional aspects correctly (including ideally without error). The app usage from the field can be used to help devise automated tests of user flows, provide more realistic timing data for the tests ("think time"), and help create automated scripts that ease the reproduction of crashes.

The recommended primary sources of data are mobile analytics and crash analytics. A useful secondary source is mining feedback from users.

Backend

Mobile analytics of user flows can be used as an input to performance and load testing scripts. Activities using the app can cause API load on the backend system(s).

Note: Mobile analytics traffic increases the load on the mobile analytics backend servers – something to consider when devising how to use mobile analytics in a mobile app.

Exploratory

Mobile analytics provides lots of usage information and meta-data on the context/settings of the mobile device that may help testers devise better interactive tests. Furthermore, the feedback is available quickly and contains lots of information so testers can adapt their testing much sooner than relying on other sources of data (or on their educated guesses, etc.)

The two primary sources of data are mobile analytics and mining feedback from users.

Smoke and Regression

Bugs should ideally live and die once and once only. However, some creep back in future releases. We can mine crash logs, as well as crashes caught by crash-reporting libraries.

Multi-Channel

Multi-channel recognises that many users expect to be able to use a mix of devices seamlessly, for instance when watching a video, composing an email, and many other tasks. Therefore, multi-channel testing for mobile apps would involve performing single, conceptual activities where the activities include at least one mobile app running on at least one mobile device.

Potentially the task could be spread across several heterogeneous devices, for instance starting on a Windows phone, continuing in turn on a BlackBerry device, an iPad, and then an Android smartphone before being completed on a laptop computer using a web app. The tests should consider latency of updates, loss of state, and other information, and the ease of being able to continue seamlessly across the various devices and implementations of the apps.

Localisation

Mobile analytics can gather information on where the app is being used and the language settings of the device and app. These various pieces of information can help devise appropriate active testing and can be used as filters to group other usage data to determine whether the app is (a) being used differently in some locales or (b) whether the app is behaving in ways that impact its use for particular locales.

The primary source would be mobile analytics if it records locale-related data; otherwise, look at app store analytics. A good secondary source is the feedback provided by users.

Offline/Online

We are not aware of mobile analytics libraries that report when the app was being used in Offline mode; however they could. The mobile analytics library would need to store and forward the relevant message(s). We might be able to infer usage if we used more sophisticated algorithms (based on calculating differences in location, for instance, between event messages received at the analytics servers).

Capacity Planning

Mobile analytics trend data (based on user flows, activities, time of day traffic, time zones, etc.) can help with capacity planning. At a macro level, usage reported in mobile analytics reports can be correlated with analysis of server-side utilisation and performance data, which may help us fine tune our capacity planning and scaling of the servers. Organisations including the Computer Measurement Group (CMG)[89] focus on capacity planning, albeit mobile apps don't seem to feature strongly.

Interaction

Users can tell us how they interact, e.g., through feedback on social media and in app store reviews. We can also use GUI-related analytics such as

---

[89] https://www.cmg.org/

heatmaps to capture interactions. Mobile analytics can be used to record other interactions, e.g., audio (voice) and movements (e.g., tilt, rotate, etc.) when suitable events are incorporated into the app.

Another form of interaction is interaction between the app and other devices, for instance with a car's electronics, wearables, and even internet-enabled coffee machines, etc.

Interruption

Android apps can register BroadcastReceivers, which receive notifications of what will become interruptions, e.g., an incoming call. Potentially, mobile analytics could report these incoming interruptions and/or relevant Android lifecycle events. With iOS it seems the OS does not allow the app the opportunity to know of, or handle, interruptions, which would make such information hard for mobile analytics to glean. Perhaps it may be possible to infer when gaps in usage could be attributed to interruptions, even on mobile platforms that don't provide the information.

Interoperability

Unless apps are using a private API (where the endpoints are known in terms of which apps are interoperating), at best we may be able to report that the app was able to interoperate with an anonymous partner. With more sophisticated detection (traffic and timing analyses) and additional testing, one might be able to identify interoperability partners though signature analysis of the protocol interactions.

In some cases, e.g., on iOS when interacting with a system service, API, etc., an app can accurately record and report interoperability with those services' APIs. For Android, by querying the device's installed apps, their registered listeners, etc., apps could potentially identify their "trading-partner".

Services and API Integrations

Services seldom have a GUI; instead, they operate in the background, albeit sometimes triggered by GUI actions and events, other times to provide ongoing capabilities. (For example, StackOverflow has various code discussions for a file download service on Android[90].) Potentially, Services may not have any GUI (e.g., Android Content Providers[91].) Instead they may serve other apps, services, and/or the system.

Network

Where network interactions are recorded and reported using mobile analytics, then the data can be mined to create suitable tests for the network aspects of mobile apps. Network analysis is unlikely to be a primary use case for mobile analytics. However, Flight Recorder has an interesting concept of recording the HTTP requests and response codes,[92] which can help us model real network traffic to make our tests more complete and more realistic.

App Store

Various services enable developers to pre-release apps to a subset of users. For those integrated into an app store we can test aspects of working with the app store framework without affecting mainstream releases. We could add additional mobile analytics into Beta releases to increase the volume and depth of the feedback that might be impractical for a full release.

Questions to consider include: How can analytics serve to get app approval? What are the top reasons why apps get rejected? How might mobile analytics help address or mitigate some of the reasons?

---

90 There are several discussions on the programmer-oriented stackoverflow.com website. For instance, http://stackoverflow. com/ questions/11932473/how-to-handle-interruptions-during-downloadinglarge-file-in-android; http://stackoverflow. com/questions/21948131/howcan-i-make-a-download-service-on-android-that-can-be-stopped-midprocess; and http:// stackoverflow.com/questions/2635786/androiddownload-large-file.

91 http://developer.android.com/guide/topics/providers/contentproviders.html

92 https://www.flightrecorder.io/feature/http-requests-and-responselogging

Installation

Google Analytics makes it possible to record installations, and automatically tracks installations on Android (unsurprisingly), and can be enabled on iOS; see: https://support.google.com/analytics/answer/3389142?hl=en. For Android, here are a couple of references to get started:

- http://help.tune.com/marketing-console/how-google-play-install-referrer-works/

- http://developers.mobileapptracking.com/testing-the-google-play-install-referrer/

Java ME[93] seems to provide the most detailed and prescriptive support for tracking installations. Java ME (which is more often used on simpler, *almost-smart* phones, has support for Installation and Deletion notification URLs. JSR-118 MIDP Documentation[94] goes into some detail on what's involved.

Note: If we're specifically tracking installations, rather than post-installation first-use of an installed app, we need to be careful not to rely (directly) on any analytics incorporated into the app.

The world of installation analytics is likely to be best understood by the app store and SDK providers (Google Play, Apple's App Store, and Windows Phone's Marketplace). One might expect each of these app stores to track installations (including errors); however, they may not share the data about failed installations externally. As developers and testers of the apps, we may therefore only learn of the successful installations.

[93] https://en.wikipedia.org/wiki/Java_Platform,_Micro_Edition

[94] http://download.oracle.com/otn-pub/jcp/midp-2.1-mreloth-JSpec/midp-2_1-mrel-spec.pdf?AuthParam=1444058557_c11bbe5f1fb64cac4116061e167b7d27

Security Analysis

Security of mobile apps is already important and is likely to become much more important in the next few years as we realise how prevalent mobile apps have become. For instance, at a European airport the automated passport gates can be remotely controlled by a mobile phone app, and – of course – mobile banking is now commonplace and widespread.

Security analysis can apply existing techniques, such as static analysis. In terms of using mobile analytics, the mobile analytics libraries are worth assessing and testing for security flaws. Apps can be configured to report various security-related information, such as when back-off algorithms are activated to protect the app from potential attackers.

Mining security vulnerability reports can help savvy teams by providing examples of how other software was vulnerable so they can fix apps the team are responsible for.

Examples of Using Feedback to Improve Testing

We have taken several examples of genuine feedback for the offline Wikipedia Reader, Kiwix.[95]

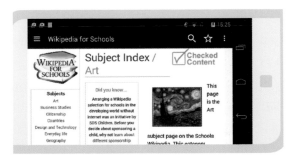

Screenshot of Kiwix for Android

95 http://kiwix.org

Kiwix enables people to interact with rich web contents, including embedded videos. It reads contents from special files, called ZIM files, where the contents are compressed to make them much smaller than the source materials.

The Android app includes an embedded web browser, a WebView, which dominates the user interface, and various capabilities and menus that resize according to the screen dimensions. The app is backwards compatible with early versions of Android, including 2.3, and is fully internationalised, to help as many users as is globally practical. The project is opensource, and can, therefore, be studied and enhanced easily.

Feedback: Cannot Copy the Content

The full comment is: *"Nice but I can't copy the content"*. The feedback is short and clear.

As copying is a feature expected by users in many apps, and one that can be immensely frustrating when it doesn't work, we could consider this a bug and one worth fixing. From a testing perspective, once we have agreed the app should support copying of content in the GUI, we can add tests for copying from Kiwix and pasting. As the content is intended to be read-only, the main place paste could be tested is using the search feature. Additional tests to paste content to other apps would be useful to help determine whether Kiwix meets the user's expectations.

Feedback: Cannot Find "World War One"!

The full comment is *"Very bad. When I typed many titles for ex 'world war one' it does not show any informations"*.

The comment is a little harder to parse, for instance "for ex" instead of the full "for example", and using "informations" as the plural form, rather than "information". Nonetheless, there is a key usability issue here – the user does not expect to have to search using the exact case of the text in the contents.

In terms of the usability issue, the app is intended to help people read contents and find content they search for. The app used exact matching, and limits this to topic searches rather than full text searches. (For technical and space reasons the app is unlikely to support full text searches in the near future.) These characteristics make the app much harder to use. The app is working as designed, but not as some users wish. Therefore, once the development team agrees to implement case-insensitive searches, tests can be added for case-insensitive searches against known content. These tests could probably be automated.

Potentially, the search could be further enhanced using fuzzy matching, for instance to accept "world war 1" as a synonym for "world war one". Search engine design and implementation are quite involved and sometimes complex topics.

"Curate's Egg" Feedback

The full comment is quite detailed and contains several overlapping pieces of feedback. *"Finally zooms properly in KitKat! However, need to [Clear Data] to resolve Force Close problem after update. When my Samsung tablet got updated to KitKat last year, I was not able to use Kiwix properly because of the incorrect zooming. Have been waiting for this fix since. However, after the 1.94 update, the app keeps force-closing. Discovered that if you go to Settings > Applications > Kiwix and then click the [Clear Cache] and [Clear Data] buttons, that fixes the crash problem".*

This is a rich source of information, including advice for other users of the Kiwix app. They have raised issues of usability and accessibility (zooming), upgrades, and the effects of an operating system update to Android KitKat (version 4.4). Android KitKat included a significant change to the embedded WebView that many apps use.[96] The revised WebView no longer reflowed text and other contents when zoomed. Although there were good reasons why Google removed this feature, the change adversely affected users who wanted or needed (in terms of accessibility) to resize contents on the screen. There was no simple fix from a programmer's perspective.

In terms of testing, there are numerous tests available, including the following:

- Pinch and Zoom on each version of Android, particularly KitKat where the embedded WebView changed technologies.

- Testing the app's functionality when the platform is upgraded. Include tests that upgrade between non-contiguous updates, for instance, where a user upgrades from 1.8 to 2.0.

- Testing the preservation of user preferences on deinstallation and reinstallation.

Strategically, it may be worth analysing crash logs to determine whether we could detect the problem from that data alone.

---

[96] A useful discussion on the security implications is http://www.androidcentral.com/android-webview-security.

Feedback: User Settings Lost on Reinstallation

A user reported that *"After uninstall/install again, it works (I just lose my favorites)".*

Again, there are a couple of spelling mistakes that may complicate automated analysis of the feedback. Users might reasonably expect that their favourites would be preserved if they uninstall and reinstall an app. After all, we might do likewise if we have problems applying an update. However, there may be limitations on how the platform (operating system installed on the device) deals with app-specific data when an app is uninstalled. Potentially, the app could store user settings and favourites in a way that would preserve them through uninstall/reinstall cycles.

Analytics might be able to provide insights into how often users follow the uninstall/reinstall cycle rather than an in-situ upgrade.

In terms of testing: Did we test if uninstalling and reinstalling preserved the favourites? Perhaps there's a latent problem, or perhaps we should set expectations if there is no workaround, etc.?

Feedback can help us understand different usage patterns, scenarios, etc. For instance, with Kiwix, several users asked questions about using data files of up to 40GB: Does the testing include tests with single large files (where a single file is around 40GB) and sharded files, where the content is split into a set of several 2GB files (used to cope with limitations in FAT32 file systems)?

We can summarise how feedback can help us improve our testing as two main aspects:

- Stuff we missed that we could and perhaps should have "caught" during testing.

- New discoveries on ways the app is being used that can enrich and tune our testing.

Driving Testing from App Store Feedback

We can start sampling by reading daily reviews for our app, and possibly also for some similar apps if we think the feedback would be relevant to help us devise tests. To scale the work we may want or need to automate the data collection. Sentiment analysis, categorisation, and mining for information of devices, etc. can all be used to provide skeletal models for us to create some appropriate tests.

- Antony Marcano proposed a novel concept of creating failing acceptance tests where practical, rather than writing a bug report.[97]

- Where usability issues are reported, consider whether running usability-evaluations would help uncover additional areas where usability can be improved.

- You may notice some devices become notorious for poor user experiences; if so, it's worth adding these models to your pool of devices to use when testing new releases.

There are several relevant research papers on mining online reviews, including: *"Retrieving and Analyzing Mobile Apps Feature Requests from Online Reviews"*[98] and *"AR-Miner: Mining Informative Reviews for Developers from Mobile App Marketplace"*[99] where researchers provide various examples of how they were able to discover relevant information including unmet performance requirements, feature requests, etc.

---

[97] Described in a topic called "The Hidden Backlog" pp. 426-427 in Agile Testing, ISBN 978-0-321-53446-0.

[98] http://ieeexplore.ieee.org/xpls/abs_all.jsp?arnumber=6624001

[99] Ravindranath, L., Nath, S., Padhye, J., Balakrishnan, H. "Automatic and ScalableFault Detection for Mobile Applications." ACM, 2014.

MINING DATA HELPS IDENTIFY INNOVATIVE WAYS TO TEST

Microsoft mined crash reports collected by the Windows Phone app store and they discovered that many apps suffered from common flaws. Over 90% of the crashes were caused by only 10% of the root causes. They then created a testbed where they used various virtual "monkeys" that were able to cause mischief for the apps to test whether the app coped well under realistic, adverse conditions. They found over 1,000 new bugs, and therefore the app developers were now able to quickly hone in on the areas worth improving in their code.[100]

Sources of data to mine include:

- Mobile analytics data (structured)

- Crash data (structured)

- Feedback (unstructured, free-form text)

Structured data is often easier to process and tends to be more data oriented. In comparison, and as examples in this chapter show, unstructured, free form text is significantly harder to process and the results are more likely to have errors of interpretation.

TEST RECOMMENDATION ENGINE

Two of the perennial challenges for software testing are (a) deciding which tests to perform from an existing pool of tests, and (b) identifying additional tests to help complement the existing tests. Research, back in 2010, considered a concept described as "**R**ecommendation **S**ystems for **S**oftware

---

100 Ravindranath, L., Nath, S., Padhye, J., Balakrishnan, H. "Automatic and Scalable Fault Detection for Mobile Applications." ACM, 2014.

Engineering" (RSSE) and how it might help software developers by making recommendations.[101] The first chapter of a book,[102] on RSSE, is a good place to learn more about the concepts involved.

Mobile analytics is able to provide a rich, ongoing source of data about how an app is being used, and as such it's worth exploring how the data could be used as part of a **T**est **R**ecommendation **E**ngine (TRE). Similarly, user feedback and crash analytics can also be incorporated to help provide recommendations of tests. The following figure indicates the main sources of information when using mobile analytics as the main source.

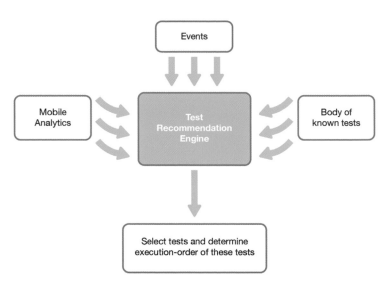

Test Recommendation Engine

Our decisions can be based on events, for instance when a new release of the app has been built successfully, or when someone reports a problem with an installed version of the app. Mobile analytics can be used as an

---

[101] Robillard, M. P., Walker, R. J., and Zimmermann, T.: "Recommendation Systems for Software Engineering." IEEE Software; 2010

[102] Robillard, P. R. and Walker, R.J.: "An Introduction to Recommendation Systems in Software Engineering." Springer, 2014.

additional source of data to augment and enhance our current decisions. The concept is of a Test Recommendation Engine (TRE), which combines information gleaned from mobile analytics with the body of known tests and inputs from various events.

The TRE could be fully automated, for instance by using machine learning, or it could involve knowledgeable "experts" such as a skilled analyst-tester.

Simple recommendations can be based on characteristics of the devices, for instance when the app starts being used on a new, previously unused, model. The importance of the new model may increase on factors such as whether it has a previously untested screen resolution or screen aspect, etc. Similarly, if there are higher error rates (as indicated by crash analytics), slower performance, or higher abandonment rates, specific testing of the app on those devices may help us determine whether there is a relationship between the model and whatever aspects are providing cause for concern.

Higher than average rates of change to data may also be worth investigating, both when the values are increasing and when they are decreasing. For instance, if a device loses popularity, that might be a valid cause for concern and – as experienced performance testers know – if performance seems to improve markedly, there may be a bug that's surfaced somewhere in the app or the supporting systems.

In terms of identifying new tests, there are several research projects where usage data and crash data have been successfully used to create new tests[103] and ways of reproducing bugs automatically.[104] These projects show some of the potential of how mobile analytics (with the usage data it can provide) and crash analytics can be used to create highly relevant automated tests.

---

[103] Linares-Vásquez, M., et al. "Mining Android App Usages for Generating Actionable GUI-based Execution Scenarios." cs.wm.edu.

[104] White, M., et al. "Generating Reproducible and Replayable Bug Reports from Android Application Crashes," 23rd IEEE International Conference on Program Comprehension (ICPC), 2015.

THRESHOLDS AND ALERTS

Once we use mobile analytics as a source of information about the usage of a mobile app we should be able to find ways to process that data on an ongoing basis to generate alerts when thresholds are crossed, for instance if the error rate exceeds a threshold, or conversely a previously popular device drops below a threshold. These alerts could provide something akin to a news feed and be used to overlay some of the charts and graphs in the reports.
We may want the alerting system to:

- Wake me when ..., and ...

- Tell me when a trend changes significantly (for instance if usage changes exponentially.)

THINGS TO CONSIDER

Mobile analytics is not a panacea, although it can help significantly, and materially, it will not "solve" our testing challenges. Here are a couple of topics worth considering.

Necessary but Not Sufficient[105]

There's more to do. For instance, we have to learn how to understand and apply the analytics to get effective results, and continually seek ways to improve the analytics.

Mobile analytics does not tell us everything, and may not even be the ideal source of information. There are other similar and complementary techniques,

---

[105] Necessary but not sufficient is a philosophical concept that can help us realise there's more needed. An interesting online resource is a video from Khan Academy.

for instance interviewing users, using heatmaps, and even using performance profiling tools.

Mobile analytics complements crash reporting, and both have a broad reach across most of the running instances of an app. They're both able to report on usage in development and testing as well as in the field. Users can volunteer additional feedback, for instance through an app store or on social media.

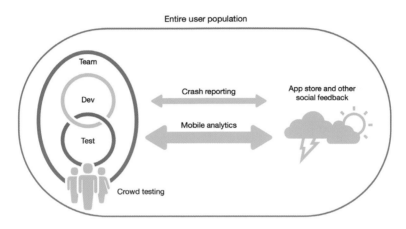

Where Mobile Analytics Fits

Notes for "Where Mobile Analytics Fits" Diagram

1. The entire user population are those who've used the app at least once and haven't deinstalled the software. Some may not have internet access, others may block the ability for the app to send feedback, while others aren't using the app currently.

2. Social feedback is also relevant to the team, including dev and test.

3. Crowd-sourced testing tends to provide some relevant information to the test team, little to the rest of the team, and the crowd testing team/company probably know more than they've explained to the test team, etc.

Mobile analytics does not report lack of use when the app is stopped. However, we may be able to infer the periods when it's not been used when events are reported each time the app is started and stopped cleanly. In some cases the stop event may not be reported (for instance, when the operating system forces the app to stop, perhaps after a crash or when the device is working too hard). If so, we may be able to infer when the app stopped. We may be able to combine crash data gathered and reported by the platform through the app store to fill in otherwise missing data. In-app analytics doesn't report when an app has been uninstalled, or removed from a device, or when a device has been wiped and reset. Again, we may be able to use industry data and guesstimates to infer when an app stopped being used.

Unknown-Unknowns and Known-Unknowns

Mobile analytics only reports the information it's designed to capture and where it has a viable connection to send the data. There will be data it does not capture and situations where it doesn't send the data. We need to keep in mind the data that isn't captured. Also, the data that is captured and resulting reports may be flawed and have bugs in them. It is worth calibrating the reports by running some internal tests. We will cover testing of mobile analytics in the next chapter.

Automation Can Degrade Outcomes

Over a decade ago, Cummings wrote a key paper[106] on ways people's performance can degrade to the detriment of the decision and the outcome as systems become more automated. We may over-trust information from analytics and over-rely on recommendations from those systems. We need to consciously guard against these biases and instincts, and perhaps there's

---

[106] Cummings, M. L.: "Automation Bias in Intelligent Time Critical Decision Support Systems," MIT, 2004; http://web.mit.edu/aeroastro/labs/ halab/papers/CummingsAIAAbias.pdf

work for us to do to find ways to compensate and adapt both the systems and our interactions with them in order to improve the decision making and outcomes.

Let's finish this chapter with another quote from Alan Page, of Microsoft: *"You are not the customer. Data helps you learn about the customer. Measure often, learn often"*.[107]

107 Page, A.: "The Mobile Application Compatibility Challenge, Mobile Deep Dive Conference," 06 Nov 2015.

YOUR FUTURE

Perhaps the time has come for you to decide what you'd like to do next?

Your app may already use mobile analytics; if so, then a good first step would be to review the outputs and reports and see what insights you glean to help you improve your testing. It might also be worth verifying that the implementation is accurate and trustworthy – we'll cover some testing aspects later in this chapter. Once you've established your baseline, then it'll be worth considering how to improve, tune, and refine the data that's being collected and reported on. Perhaps another library or technique would be worth investing in?

For apps that don't include mobile analytics, there are various options. Perhaps one of the free-to-use options would be worth considering, or HP's AppPulse Mobile, with its auto-integration, might also be worth trying. Technically, you can experiment and evaluate with pre-release versions of your app, rather than immediately having to incorporate mobile analytics and launch the app to end users through the app store. We'll provide tips for evaluating libraries later in this chapter.

Alternatively, if you're willing to work with source code, and have more flexibility, you might consider experimenting with adding mobile analytics to one or two opensource or example apps (most mobile SDKs include sample apps that demonstrate the capabilities of the tools and the platform).

For enterprise mobile apps, it may be worth working with the current distribution channels and customer support to find ways to improve the communication and information gathering from your enterprise customers. There may be various commercial and practical limitations to what data can be collected and how the data would be processed and made available for you to analyse.

EXAMPLES OF MOBILE ANALYTICS LIBRARIES

There are a plethora of choices available, ranging from free fully opensource offerings such as Countly[108], where both the client and server libraries are freely available, to high-end paid-for commercial offerings.

If you would like to compare several libraries, a good strategy might be to seek diversity in the product offerings. For instance, a market leader, an opensource project, one that does heatmapping, an innovative offering, and one that focuses on the user. Here are three examples we have picked to illustrate this book.

AppPulse Mobile

AppPulse Mobile[109] could be considered innovative, particularly for the way it can be easily added to mobile apps without any additional software needing to be written to integrate the library. Here is a brief summary of various characteristics.

---

[108] https://count.ly/

[109] https://saas.hpe.com/software/AppPulse-mobile

- Innovative black-box approach to integrating the library that automatically identifies and generates analytics events. Supports tracking actions in embedded WebViews.

- The reports include a "FunDex score", provide trends, and enable easy filtering of the data.

- AppPulse Mobile supports iOS and Android, and the development tools are supported on Windows and OS X.

- There is good support for privacy. For instance, to prevent tracking of sensitive information, and it enables developers to easily offer an opt-in for the end users.

AppPulse Mobile FunDex Score

AppPulse UI Actions

AppPulse Mobile takes a user-centric approach, for instance FunDex captures various aspects of the Quality of Experience as experienced by users.

Mixpanel

Mixpanel[110] is a popular product that includes both mobile analytics and an A/B experimentation platform. While it needs to be manually integrated into an app, once it's been integrated it offers a visual way to tag events without needing to write more code. The following screenshot shows the visual editor after adding several tags to the Kiwix app.

Mixpanel Visual Tags Added

[110] https://mixpanel.com/

However, there seem to be various limitations of the visual tagging. For instance, the dropdown menu, which was actually showing on the device, wasn't recognised. Here's what was on the device:

Dropdown Menu Not Recognised

Also, interactions with the WebView, where the contents are displayed, did not seem to be recognised.

Timestamps in the reports are based on the device's date and time rather than on a common system time. This may make comparisons based on local time easier; for instance, do users in different timezones all start using the app around 8am? However, if the device's clock is materially incorrect, for instance a day, then the events may be allocated to the wrong date. Modelling the load on the servers may be problematic as the device timestamps would need to be mapped to a common time, such as UTC.

Overall, Mixpanel provides a rich and mature set of features with specific integrations for web, BlackBerry 10, iOS, and Android apps. The clients are available as opensource projects (https://github.com/mixpanel/) which makes them easy to customise, for instance to preserve analytics data on the device for extended periods.

Countly

Countly[108] is unusual for several reasons: it's fully opensource, and you can easily host the service privately[111] so you have complete control of the environment and data. Of course, you'll then be responsible for maintaining and protecting the servers and the service in terms of security, performance, and availability. Hardcore projects can choose to extend the analytics so it collects precisely the data that's relevant.

Countly supports many more platforms, including Android, BlackBerry, iOS, and Windows Phone, so it may be on the shortlist for apps that need to be supported across these platforms. Countly is also designed with rich server APIs, both to post and retrieve data, allowing for custom clients and automated data extraction.

Getting started is a little more cumbersome, as the documentation for Android missed some key configuration details needed to build the app. The example project was hard to find and also failed to compile. However, for people who would like the flexibility, and are willing to spend some more time dealing with technical intricacies, Countly may suit their needs.

108 https://count.ly/

111 Free for non-commercial, personal or in-company use: https://count.ly/community-edition/.

TIPS AND TRAPS

Like most things in life, there are tradeoffs and complications to consider when incorporating mobile analytics into your app.

Our Responsibilities

We have various responsibilities. Some may be implicit, such as being good custodians and trusted guardians on behalf of the end users and other stakeholders. Can users trust us in terms of their privacy and data costs? Consider how we can involve the users in decisions about their data. Do we give them the ability to make informed consent?

As testers and software engineers we need to establish whether the library and service are sufficiently trustworthy in terms of providing accurate, timely, and complete results. What happens when things go wrong, for instance, if data is lost, a service fails, etc.? Do we have mitigation plans, and how well have they been tested?

From our organisation's perspective, we may bind the organisation to various responsibilities by the time we've clicked-though a licence agreement to download the "free trial" software. Part of due diligence includes the legal aspects. We cover due diligence later in this chapter.

Lean Selection Criteria

We may start with little idea of how to select the most appropriate library (or libraries) for our context. Rushing to pick a library is likely to be counterproductive later on (*"buy in haste, repent at leisure"*). Conversely, taking a long time might also be counterproductive and cause the initiative to atrophy. Instead, aim to find ways to maximise your learning and discovery while avoiding some of the "gotchas" (we will cover these later on).

Principles from lean software development can help us to experiment and learn quickly and iteratively. Aim to craft mini experiments that minimise your effort to maximise your learning and discovery, quickly. For instance, you may be able to integrate a library in a test build of an existing app (either one of ours or an opensource one). Ask questions and do some initial research online, including on websites such as http://stackoverflow.com/, to learn what developers' experiences are. For instance, http://stackoverflow.com/search?q=mixpanel+android currently has 99 results, including several technical challenges. Also, SourceDNA provides statistics on which apps use various ad[112] and analytics libraries (https://sourcedna.com/stats/), and SafeDK provides complementary information. Again, here's the example for mixpanel: http://www.safedk.com/sdks/mixpanel-mixpanel.

At this stage, try not to get bogged down with complex or time-consuming evaluations. Also, if the sign-up conditions are onerous, there are plenty of other competing options you can try as part of your initial experiments. Once you've learned more, you'll have a better perspective on whether or not to invest the time with the more involved options.

Don't Get Trapped

Although evaluating and selecting a mobile analytics library may be involved, there's a risk that separating from a provider will be at least as time-consuming and involved, especially if you've not considered the "divorce" when selecting the library. There are various facets to consider, including technical, business, and legal.

Technically, the API provided by each library tends to be unique, and each offers different features, so replacing one with another is likely to involve both

---

[112] Ad is a common term for Advertising.

code changes and changes to the data that's reported. Segment[113] provides a common API that integrates with over 40 analytics libraries at the time of writing. They remove much of the technical headache, and may enable you to find workable solutions for maintaining key data provided you are willing to pick a set of libraries that can capture the data you want to preserve.

Quite often organisations establish internal business measures and objectives based on the analytics, for instance sales and marketing targets where removing or replacing the library may cause significant problems and even affect senior people's bonuses – when people's income is at risk they may become very defensive! We recommend you consider aspects such as data ownership: Who owns the data generated by your app? How much of the data and results would you have access to when you're using the service[114] and post termination? How easily can you access and archive the data? What are your backout plans so you can stop using a library cleanly and without regret?

From a legal perspective, there may be contractual issues to consider and data privacy aspects for the data a provider has captured. Perhaps the equivalent of a prenuptial agreement, even if it's only written for internal use, would help reduce any regrets if you decide to stop using a service in the future.

Tips to Get Started

Testers and testing can help from the initial stages of an evaluation through to testing a full implementation. We will cover this topic in more detail later in this chapter, in the Testing Mobile Analytics section.

Start by evaluating the claims of the vendors. From evaluating their claims you'll obtain a good overview of features and be able to use these to

---

[113] https://segment.com/

[114] Some analytics services include an API to query and obtain data from the analytics servers. These include Countly and HP AppPulse Mobile.

consider which of these features suit the needs of your project. Consider the trustworthiness of the vendor and their products. Other "desk research" can include skimming reading the entire licence agreement for problematic clauses and applying the lean selection criteria mentioned earlier.

Next, establish a small pilot where you incorporate various libraries into one of your apps, and try using the app to observe the behaviours of the app with the libraries. You could also try incorporating libraries into example apps and/or opensource apps.

Finally, use a timeline to consider the suitability of potential libraries over various periods, ranging from 1 day, 1 month, 1 year, and 5 years.

TAKE YOUR PICK

When you're aware of what the various offerings provide, their strengths, and weaknesses, you should be able to shortlist candidates to incorporate into your mobile apps.

Considerations for evaluating libraries include the following:

- Richness of events and the data they provide.

- Ability to generate custom events and send custom data.

- Support for your app types (native, composite, hybrid, web) and platforms.

    - First, consider the platform(s) you expect you will need to support, for instance iOS, Android, Windows Phone, etc.

    - In addition, the technologies used to implement the app are also important, particularly where they use a web browser as part of the app, such as a WebView in Android or iOS. Some mobile analytics tools do not capture key aspects of what's happening in the web browser, which could mean major aspects of your app go unrecorded and unreported.

- Behaviours, including what happens when no internet connection is available. What does the library do? Does it store and forward the data once the connection is available? Does it report summary data instead, or are the events discarded and unreported?

- Security hygiene: How does the provider address the security of the app, the data and the service?

- Popularity of the library and related product. There may be significantly more information available about more popular offerings, which reduce the risk of facing problems "on your own".

TESTING MOBILE ANALYTICS

As we mentioned earlier in this chapter, testing the mobile analytics is very important, particularly if the team and organisation want to rely on the data and insights. As an organisation, we also need to comply with legal and contractual details and implement a trustworthy system. Also, to maximise the return on our investment of time, money, trust, resources, and network bandwidth, etc., it's worth investing the time to test as part of our acceptance criteria of the potential libraries and our integration.

To follow are some common core tests worth considering. More detailed testing guidelines to help assess and test mobile analytics libraries are freely available online at https://github.com/julianharty/testing-mobile-analytics.

Numbers

Can the overall service count correctly? Can we trust the numbers it provides? (At least one commercial product had multiple failures for this straightforward test.)

- Do the reports accurately reflect 0, 1, 2, several, and many concurrent sessions? Before the library is active, the counts should all be zero, and when the system is idle, the load should show as zero.

- When does it count a new session? For instance, when the app is suspended and resumed? After idle periods? And, when is the session deemed to be over? Does the behaviour and the algorithm they use vary from one platform to another? Consider, there's no guarantee the behaviour will be identical across their implementations.

Do the Messages Get Delivered, and, If So, When?

Ultimately, mobile analytics needs to forward data from the app to where it can be processed and used. However, libraries vary in their behaviours, particularly when there isn't a direct, reliable connection from the app to the collection point. Perhaps you don't mind if some data doesn't arrive. However, it's at least worth understanding the circumstances where you can trust the library to deliver the data, when you know it will not do so, and any areas where the behaviour is unpredictable. Try to run tests for the following networks:

- **No network**: the device may be in flight mode, or simply without a data connection. Access may be disabled by policy, for instance if the device is roaming in another country and the user doesn't want to pay for any additional data service.

- **A closed network**: the device can be on a local network that doesn't have access to the internet. Perhaps access to the analytics server is blocked by a proxy server or firewall.

- **With a proxy server in the loop**: Does the library (and your app) honour proxy server settings on the device? (Android apps were known for not doing so, for various reasons.)

- **An open network**: The device is connected with access to the internet. What's the latency and how quickly and completely does it catch up if the library has a backlog of events waiting to be sent?

Latency is important, both in terms of forwarding the data and in the reporting aspects.

Completeness

For libraries that are added automatically, how completely do they cover the functionality of the app? Is the data sufficiently rich and distinct to be useful? When libraries are added explicitly, review the completeness of the API and determine how well the library can communicate the data you want to know. Virtually all libraries also capture and report data about the device and its settings, for instance the model, locale setting, and active language on the device. This data can help improve the quality of analysis and testing, so it's important to check if it's also complete and accurate.

Efficiency

Efficiency of the transmissions is an important acceptance criteria; after all, some popular apps can send over 10 billion events per day from active user sessions. Therefore, measure the data volumes, the number, and frequency of the events to assess the aggregate load. Some providers either can't support these volumes or charge significant fees to do so.

There are debates on whether sampling by the provider would be adequate and acceptable in terms of the accuracy of the analysis and reporting.

Therefore, you'd be wise to do some research and make a considered decision on whether to use a library that uses sampling.

Remember that individual users may be paying for the costs of the data in some cases, and they are also more likely to reduce or stop using apps that consume excessive resources. Network traffic also uses battery power, so there may be sweetspots in terms of the bundling algorithm(s) used by the mobile library (which decide tradeoffs such as efficiency, batching, and latency).

In summary, we could use the concept of an environmental impact of each library in terms of the resources it uses, and how efficiently it uses them.

Security, Privacy, and Confidentiality

We make no apology for mentioning confidentiality and privacy explicitly, although some may consider them part of security. Both topics are important from a user's perspective and possibly for other stakeholders involved in the app. We recommend doing a security review of the service, the library, and the product offering.

Read the legal terms and be willing to challenge or question what they say, their software, and what they do. Are they trying to hide or avoid aspects that would be material to you? Your trustworthiness is based on their trustworthiness. Too many companies have had security failures for us to rely on a "trust us" model. We particularly need to consider data that might identify a person, data leakage, what third parties *do* and *don't* commit to doing with the data they gather from the app, etc. A very helpful book is *Ethics of Big Data*[115] as it covers these and other related topics in a clear, readable manner.

---

[115] Davis, K. with Patterson, D.: Ethics of Big Data, O'Reilly, 2012. ISBN 978-1-449-31179-7.

Paradoxically, openness of the product offering is important. Several providers have made their client libraries available as opensource to make it easier for developers and their organisations to ascertain the behaviours and to reduce the likelihood of unknown, undesirable behaviours in a library.

Globalisation

Many mobile apps are used by geographically and linguistically diverse populations of users so mobile analytics needs to be capable of supporting both these aspects of the usage; otherwise the data will be less complete and possibly less accurate – therefore less valuable.

There are two main considerations:

- Timezones and

- Languages and locales. These include Right-To-Left (RTL) and the more commonplace Left-To-Right (LTR) languages.

RTL languages are extremely likely to expose limitations and flaws, particularly for teams who are new to implementing support for them in their mobile apps.

Summary of the Testing

We can summarise the aims of testing to establish *the truth, the whole truth, and nothing but the truth.*[116]

Qualities of the App with the Additional Libraries and Integration Code

We can, and probably should, assess the qualities of the integrated app. After all, from the user's perspective, we are ultimately responsible for the overall

---

[116] A subset of the oaths sworn in various courts of law; https://en. wikipedia.org/wiki/Sworn_testimony.

quality regardless of whose software we're using in the app. SafeDK[117] have several relevant blog posts[118] on this topic.

For any source code, including opensource code if provided (as some mobile analytics do) we can assess qualities such as maintainability and portability. It's also worth considering how you will manage and incorporate updates to the libraries (a) in terms of the code integration and (b) when the reported data changes.

INTEGRATING MOBILE ANALYTICS

There are several stages to integrating mobile analytics into an app. These include assessing and testing the library, and understanding the effects of incorporating it. In parallel, we need to design events and map relevant screens to capture the information we want to report on.

Designing Events

One of the key implementation challenges is designing the events to maximise the fit between the data we would like to obtain and how much we are able to capture.

We will often use existing API calls, where practical, as these are likely to be supported in the longer term, and are also available in the standard reports offered by the analytics service (the website where we can view the reports).

However, we will often want to record data that isn't handled by specific API calls.

---

[117] http://www.safedk.com/

[118] SafeDK blog posts cover performance (http://blog.safedk.com/technology/what-you-should-know-about-your-sdks-and-your-app-starttime/), and security (http://blog.safedk.com/sdk-economy/do-you-knowwhat- your-sdks-did-last-summer/).

Many of the analytics frameworks provide a way to report custom events, in some products, they treat everything as a custom event, which at least makes the decision of what to use easier. JSON is a popular data structure supported by the respective "custom" API call. Thankfully, there are a wide range of software tools to both generate and work with JSON formatted data. Consider how to report the contents of the custom events, and evaluate their effectiveness and usefulness throughout the reporting and analysis processes.

As a tip, make sure each event is distinct and easy to recognise correctly in the recorded data and reports. Don't use localised text in the event name, otherwise you can end up with reconciliation problems trying to map these events to common events such as the "Registration Screen". Instead, record the locale of an app at startup and if it's changed while the app is being used.

A/B Testing

In addition to investigating mobile analytics, an orthogonal approach is to consider A/B testing frameworks for mobile apps. They enable lighter-weight experiments in the field. Mobile analytics helps to capture various effects of the experiments.

One of the most prominent products for A/B testing is Optimizely.[119] They provide a wide range of resources online, for instance https://www.optimizely.com/resources/, and are worth studying to provide additional perspective on ways mobile analytics fit into the overall ecosystem. Optimizely also integrates with various mobile analytics product offerings.

---

[119] https://www.optimizely.com/

WORDS TO THE WISE

Here are some topics to ponder when considering how to integrate and implement mobile analytics:

- Do no harm. To varying degrees, mobile apps can affect people's lives. When implementing mobile analytics, we need to consider the risk of doing harm. There may also be unintended consequences or side effects worth mitigating.

- Do as you would be done by, protect people's privacy, and keep the costs down. One way to protect privacy is to minimise the data that is collected, and to consider ways to delete it as soon as practical. There may be legal and commercial factors to consider where specialist advice is necessary. Furthermore, if the analytics are provided by a third party, you may have lost control of what happens with the data. *Ethics of Big Data*[115] discusses this topic in depth.

- Minimise footprint of using mobile analytics: in the app and in use.

- Act in haste, repent at leisure. Divorce is hard and messy, even when you want to stop using a provider of mobile analytics.

- Be willing to question absurd decisions. "Misunderstanding caused by silence.... In the course of the teleconference during which the final decision to launch the shuttle was taken, several people, who were aware of the malfunction of the joints, remained silent".[120]

---

[115] Davis, K. with Patterson, D.: Ethics of Big Data, O'Reilly, 2012. ISBN 978-1-449-31179-7.

[120] http://christian.morel5.perso.sfr.fr/English%20report.pdf

Due Diligence

Due diligence enables us to investigate what does and doesn't exist and the state of affairs in terms of the software we release and the related services used to support the apps. When we perform due diligence, we are likely to find areas worth improving, including the development process, the product, the testing, and how the app, and related systems, behave in use.

One of the longer term aspects of due diligence is related to the legal aspects. Software is an unusual domain where license agreements are created to minimise risk exposure for providers, yet they are often ignored by users who find the fastest way to ignore them despite the long-term consequences of doing so. Today, many apps are buggy; new releases acknowledge bug fixes, and the testing is known to be inadequate by the development teams. The legal environment of who is responsible for what is unclear in terms of liability, ownership of data, permissions to do stuff, etc., especially where apps are available and used internationally.

The law eventually catches up with novel industries as they start to mature. This happened with websites, music sharing, cookies, and reporting of security breaches. Data collection by mobile apps, including mobile analytics, is a relatively new area in terms of the legal aspects and implications. Some recent discussions on the implications of software for robots may illuminate some of the concepts and concerns. For instance, who would be liable for leakage of data gathered by a mobile analytics library, or where tracking data was abused? Professor Ryan Calo, professor of law at the University of Washington, was recently interviewed on BBC Radio[121], where he grappled with similar questions, such as: Who is to blame when robots go wrong? He also explained about app stores for robots.[122]

---

[121] http://www.bbc.co.uk/programmes/p0325fb6

[122] Jobs for Robots

OVER TO YOU

We hope you have enjoyed reading this book and found at least a couple of interesting ideas worth considering and applying for your mobile apps. Please tell us about your experiences and progress. Also, we appreciate feedback on this book, which is still incomplete even though it grew to be over three times the size we first envisaged.

Contact Us:
http://www.themobileanalyticsplaybook.com/

APPENDIX: FURTHER READING

There is much more information available that can help you test your mobile apps more effectively and efficiently.

ACADEMIC RESEARCH

Here are various research papers to get you started. These papers are written in what may be an unfamiliar style. However, once you learn to decode them, they provide lots of clues and evidence.

- *Revisiting Prior Empirical Findings For Mobile Apps. An Empirical Case Study on the 15 Most Popular Open-Source Android Apps.*[123] (For instance, 11 of the 15 projects had no automated tests.)

- *Understanding the Test Automation Culture of App Developers.*[124] (As an example, they found over 85% of the Android apps they reviewed had no automated test cases at all.)

---

[123] http://sailhome.cs.queensu.ca/~mdsyer/wp-content/uploads/2013/ 09/Revisiting-Prior-Empirical-Findings-For-Mobile-Apps-An-Empirical- Case-Study-on-the-15-Most-Popular-Open-Source-Android-Apps.pdf

[124] http://thomas-zimmermann.com/publications/files/kochhar-icst-2015.pdf

- *App Quality Alliance*[125] provides useful sources of testing ideas for various platforms, and for testing Accessibility.

- *Effectiveness of Multi-device Testing Mobile Applications.*[126] (5 devices are enough to find at least 4 out of 5 detected bugs. The variations in OS version had the largest chance of finding the bugs.)

- *How to Smash the Next Billion Mobile App Bugs?*[127] (A good overview of Microsoft Research's work using various test monkeys to automatically find various types of bugs quickly and inexpensively.)

Finding Academic Papers
Google Scholar is able to find legitimate, freely available copies of many academic papers: https://scholar.google.com/.

BOOKS

All these books are very readable and provide thought-provoking ideas we may be able to apply to what we do.

- *How to measure anything*, 3rd ed. ISBN 978-1-118-53927-9 (The book has a supporting website http://www.howtomeasureanything.com/.)

There are several good books on analytics, including:

- *Analytics at Work*, ISBN 978-1422177693

- *Predictive Analytics*, ISBN 978-1118356852

---

[125] http://www.appqualityalliance.org/resources

[126] http://core.ecu.edu/STRG/publications/Vilkomir-MobileSoft-2015-proceedings.pdf

[127] http://niclane.org/pubs/getmobile_smash.pdf

O'Reilly publishes numerous free, short books including at least 20 on Big Data. You need to register online to read these books. They are available at http://www.oreilly.com/data/free/. They also have several relevant short books for purchase including:

- *Ethics of Big Data*, ISBN 978-1-449-31179-7

- *Thinking with Data*, ISBN 978-1-449-36293-5

ARTICLES

- Good advice to focus your attention on the purpose of app analytics (http://info.localytics.com/blog/purpose-powered-app-analytics) and focus on increasing engagement (http://techcrunch.com/2011/03/15/mobile-app-users-are-both-fickle-and-loyal-study/).

- Michael Wu writes a very relevant and readable blog on various topics including Big Data and Analytics. Here are some examples:

    ○ *Descriptive Analytics.*[128]

    ○ *Predictive Analytics.*[129]

    ○ *From Descriptive to Prescriptive Analytics.*[130]

    ○ *Finding Signal in the Noise.*[131]

---

[128] http://community.lithium.com/t5/Science-of-Social-blog/Big-Data-Reduction-1-Descriptive-Analytics/ba-p/77766

[129] http://community.lithium.com/t5/Science-of-Social-blog/Big-Data-Reduction-2-Understanding-Predictive-Analytics/ba-p/79616

[130] http://community.lithium.com/t5/Science-of-Social-blog/Big-Data-Reduction-3-From-Descriptive-to-Prescriptive/ba-p/81556 1

[131] http://community.lithium.com/t5/Science-of-Social-blog/The-Key-to-Insight-Discovery-Where-to-Look-in-Big-Data-to-Find/ba-p/70116